THE BABE RUTH ERA

Old-Time BASEBALL TRIVIA

KERRY BANKS

GREYSTONE BOOKS

Douglas & McIntyre

VANCOUVER/TORONTO

For my mother, Elizabeth, who brought me into the world.

Greystone Books
A division of Douglas & McIntyre Ltd.
1615 Venables Street
Vancouver, British Columbia V5L 2H1

Canadian Cataloguing in Publication Data

Banks, Kerry, 1952–
    The Babe Ruth era

    ISBN 1-55054-613-9

    1. Baseball—History—Miscellanea. I. Title
GV867.3.B345 1998   796.357′09   C97-911099-8

Editing by John Eerkes
Cover and text design by Peter Cocking
Front cover photograph courtesy *The Sporting News*
Back cover photograph courtesy National Baseball Hall of Fame Library, Cooperstown, N.Y.
Printed and bound in Canada by Best Book Manufacturers

Every reasonable effort has been taken to trace the ownership of copyrighted visual material. Information that will enable the publisher to rectify any reference or credit is welcome.

The publisher gratefully acknowledges the assistance of the Canada Council for the Arts and of the British Columbia Ministry of Tourism, Small Business and Culture.

Contents

PREFACE

On January 3, 1920, the Boston Red Sox sold Babe Ruth to the New York Yankees and baseball changed forever. In Boston, Ruth had been a pitcher and part-time outfielder. In New York, he became a full-time outfielder and everyday sensation. Ruth took baseball by storm in 1920, slamming a record-breaking 54 home runs, more than any other team in the American League. It wasn't just the number of balls he belted over the fence that electrified fans, but the incredible distances they traveled. A new word, "Ruthian," meaning colossal or with great power, entered the American lexicon.

Ruth's impact was dramatic. Before his arrival in New York, baseball was a pitching-dominated game. Teams scratched out one run at a time with place hitting, sacrifice bunts, base stealing and hit-and-run plays. A batter was supposed to protect the plate, to get a piece of the ball at all costs. Ruth dispensed with all that science and strategy. For him, a strike-out was no disgrace, only a temporary setback. His game was simpler and more destructive. Said Ruth: "I swing big, with everything I've got. I hit big or I miss big. I like to live as big as I can."

Thanks to Ruth's charisma, the Yankees drew more than one million spectators in 1920, setting a new major-league attendance record. With dollar signs dancing in their eyes, baseball owners revamped the game to give fans more offense. They passed legislation outlawing trick pitches and juiced up the ball. Hitters switched to lighter, thinner-handled bats and began swinging for the fences, and the scoreboards lit up with runs.

The power-hitting revolution would be carried on by such fabled sluggers as Lou Gehrig, Jimmie Foxx, Mel Ott, Hank Greenberg, Joe DiMaggio and Ted Williams. Yet, as talented as these performers were, they all played in the oversize shadow of that big, fat hellraiser in Yankee pinstripes. It was Babe Ruth's era.

KERRY BANKS
January 1998

1

Babe Ruth:
His booming bat
changed
baseball forever.

Chapter One

CLEARING THE BASES

The revelation that the 1919 World Series had been fixed shook baseball to the core and frightened club owners. In an attempt to restore the game's integrity, the owners appointed Kenesaw Mountain Landis, an egotistical and famously tough 54-year-old federal judge, as commissioner and granted him absolute authority. While Landis applied his brand of stern justice to cleaning up the game's darker elements, Babe Ruth was single-handedly restoring fans' faith on the diamond. Installed in the New York Yankees outfield in 1920, Ruth awed the nation with his thunderous hitting. His titanic batting feats, magnetic personality and flamboyant lifestyle captivated America and propelled baseball into a golden age.

(Answers are on page 8)

1.1   **On January 3, 1920, Boston Red Sox owner Harry Frazee sold Babe Ruth to the New York Yankees for $125,000 and a $300,000 loan. Why did Frazee need the money?**
A. To pay off gambling debts
B. To refurbish Fenway Park
C. To produce Broadway plays
D. To finance construction of a cruise ship

1.2 **In 1921, eight Chicago White Sox players went on trial for their role in rigging the 1919 World Series. What was the verdict?**

A. All were found guilty

B. All but one were found guilty

C. All were found not guilty

D. There was no verdict; the trial was suspended

1.3 **Joe DiMaggio was known as "the Yankee Clipper." What type of transportation was he named after?**

A. A train

B. A boat

C. An automobile

D. An airplane

1.4 **In 1920, Ray Chapman of the Cleveland Indians died after being hit in the head by a pitched ball. Which hurler delivered the fateful pitch?**

A. Hooks Dauss of the Tigers

B. Carl Mays of the Yankees

C. Red Faber of the White Sox

D. Bullet Joe Bush of the Red Sox

1.5 **In 1941, Ted Williams became the last American Leaguer to hit .400. Who was the last National Leaguer to break the barrier?**

A. Paul Waner

B. Bill Terry

C. Chuck Klein

D. Rogers Hornsby

1.6 **What was doubly remarkable about Ty Cobb's .401 batting average with the Detroit Tigers in 1922?**

A. He was 35 years old

B. He was also the Tigers' manager

C. He didn't win the batting crown

D. All of the above

1.7   **What prompted the owners of the New York Yankees to build Yankee Stadium in 1922?**
A. They received an interest-free loan
B. The Yankees' home park burned down
C. The Yankees were evicted from their home park
D. They needed a larger stadium to accommodate the huge crowds Babe Ruth was attracting

1.8   **In what year did Babe Ruth become the majors' all-time home run leader?**
A. 1921
B. 1924
C. 1927
D. 1930

1.9   **Who was the first player-manager to pilot his club to a pennant and win the MVP Award in the same year?**
A. Rogers Hornsby of the Cubs
B. Frankie Frisch of the Cardinals
C. Joe Cronin of the Senators
D. Mickey Cochrane of the Tigers

1.10 **In 1935, Cleveland Indians scout Cy Slapnicka signed teenage phenom Bob Feller to a major-league contract. What was Feller's bonus for signing?**
A. $1
B. $1,000
C. $10,000
D. $100,000

1.11 **Who hit the fabled "homer in the gloamin" in 1938?**
A. Arky Vaughan of the Pirates
B. Gabby Hartnett of the Cubs
C. Jimmy Ripple of the Giants
D. Tommy Henrich of the Yankees

1.12   Which pair of brothers were known as "Big Poison" and
"Little Poison"?
A. Dizzy and Paul Dean
B. Joe and Dom DiMaggio
C. Paul and Lloyd Waner
D. Virgil and Jesse Barnes

1.13   Which ballpark's dollhouse dimensions made it a left-handed
hitters' paradise?
A. Cleveland's League Park
B. Philadelphia's Baker Bowl
C. Pittsburgh's Forbes Field
D. Cincinnati's Crosley Field

1.14   The New York Yankees won ten world titles from 1920 to
1945. What was the Yankees' won–lost record in their
ten Series triumphs?
A. 40–7
B. 40–12
C. 40–17
D. 40–22

1.15   When Lou Gehrig left the Yankee lineup on May 2, 1939, after a
record 2,130 consecutive games, who replaced him at first base?
A. Jake Powell
B. Babe Dahlgren
C. Charlie Keller
D. Bill Knickerbocker

1.16   Who was the era's only unanimous choice as MVP?
A. Jimmie Foxx in 1932
B. Dizzy Dean in 1934
C. Hank Greenberg in 1935
D. Lou Gehrig in 1936

1.17 **Which pitcher was given the starting assignment in five of the first six All-Star games?**
A. Lefty Gomez
B. Carl Hubbell
C. Dizzy Dean
D. Lefty Grove

1.18 **Most teams suffered a decline in attendance during the Depression years. The St. Louis Browns fared worst of all. What was the Browns' average attendance per game at its lowest ebb?**
A. 1,000
B. 3,000
C. 5,000
D. 7,000

1.19 **After being voted MVP of the Southern Association in 1944, which one-armed outfielder was promoted to the majors in 1945, to become the only one-armed position player in big-league annals?**
A. Pete Gray of the Browns
B. Bud Metheny of the Yankees
C. Oris Hockett of the White Sox
D. Danny Gardella of the Giants

1.20 **Who played in the most World Series games between 1920 and 1945?**
A. Babe Ruth
B. Bill Dickey
C. Goose Goslin
D. Frankie Frisch

Answers

CLEARING THE BASES

1.1 C. To produce Broadway plays

Baseball was merely a sideline for Harry Frazee. His true passion was Broadway, and he viewed the Red Sox as a source of financing for his theatrical operations. Soon after buying the Sox in 1917, he began selling his players to bankroll a series of failed Broadway ventures. The 1920 sale of Babe Ruth for $125,000 provided a short-term windfall for Frazee, but it was a long-term disaster for Boston. Before Ruth's exit, the Red Sox had won five World Series; they have not won one since. The key to the deal for Frazee was a $300,000 loan he obtained from Yankee owner Colonel Jacob Ruppert. Since Ruppert would not agree to the loan without some form of security and since the only thing of value Frazee owned was Fenway Park, Ruppert acquired the mortgage on the Red Sox's stadium. If not illegal, the arrangement was totally unethical. Frazee's musicals continued to bomb and he continued selling his star players to his new landlord, turning the BoSox into an AL doormat. But Frazee prospered. He sold the club for $1.5 million in 1923, and two years later he struck gold with his hit Broadway play *No No Nanette*.

1.2 C. All were found not guilty

The Chicago White Sox were vying for the 1920 pennant when a grand jury was convened in late September to look into allegations that some White Sox players had conspired with gamblers to throw the 1919 World Series. Three White Sox stars—Eddie Cicotte, Joe Jackson and Lefty Williams—confessed to accepting bribes and implicated five others. Owner Charles Comiskey

8

CLEARING THE BASES: ANSWERS

promptly suspended the eight players and the Sox slipped to second, finishing two games behind the Cleveland Indians. When the trial finally began on July 5, 1921, the prosecution's case suffered a setback when the confessions and waivers of immunity signed by Cicotte, Jackson and Williams mysteriously disappeared and the three recanted their confessions. The prosecution demanded five-year prison terms and $2,000 fines for the eight players. The defense argued, among other things, that the players' contracts didn't require that they try to win ballgames. The jury deliberated two hours before returning with a "not guilty" verdict. Two days later, baseball commissioner Kenesaw Mountain Landis, ignoring the acquittal, banned the eight players for life. Despite several appeals, Eddie Cicotte, Joe Jackson, Lefty Williams, Chick Gandil, Swede Risberg, Fred McMullin, Happy Felsch and Buck Weaver never played in the majors again.

1.3 **B. A boat**
Yankee radio broadcaster Arch McDonald pinned "the Yankee Clipper" tag on DiMaggio in 1937. The graceful way that the Yankee outfielder would glide across the grass in pursuit of fly balls reminded McDonald of the elegant sailing ships that used to traverse the Atlantic Ocean, so he began calling DiMaggio "the Yankee Clipper." It soon became a household term.

1.4 **B. Carl Mays of the Yankees**
On a misty afternoon on August 16, 1920, the Yankees met the Indians at the Polo Grounds. Before the game was done, the day got much darker. In the fifth inning, Yankee pitcher Carl Mays unleashed a fastball that hit Indians shortstop Ray Chapman in the head with a resounding crack. Chapman crumpled to the ground and had to be carried off the field. In the clubhouse, awaiting an ambulance, he mumbled repeatedly, "Ring. Ring. Katy's ring." Trainer Percy Smallwood retrieved Chapman's wedding ring, which he'd been holding for safekeeping, and slipped it on Chapman's finger. A look of relief crossed the shortstop's face as he lapsed into unconsciousness. Chapman died the next morning after an operation to remove pieces of bone from his brain. His death caused an uproar. The Cleveland papers called for Mays to

be banished from baseball, and some players talked about refusing to play against him. But the boycott never materialized and no disciplinary action was taken against Mays, who denied any intent to injure. Amazingly, the tragedy seemed to have little effect on the Yankee hurler, who pitched a shutout in his next start and finished the year with a 26–11 record. But Mays's errant fastball would claim another victim. Chapman's despondent widow, Kathleen, who never again attended a baseball game, committed suicide in 1928.

1.5   B. Bill Terry

The Giants' first baseman retired with a career batting average of .341, so Terry was obviously a talented hitter, but his .401 average in 1930 is tainted because it occurred during a year when, thanks to a suspiciously lively ball, hitting records fell like tenpins. Terry is the last National Leaguer to crack the .400 barrier and the only NL player besides Rogers Hornsby (who did it three times) to manage the feat in the 20th century.

1.6   D. All of the above

At 35, Ty Cobb was one of the oldest players in the majors in 1922, but nothing about his play suggested he was over the hill. In addition to handling managing duties, Cobb batted .401, with 99 runs, 42 doubles, 16 triples and 99 RBI. Despite his .401 average, Cobb was denied the AL batting crown by the Browns' George Sisler, who hit a sizzling .420. Cobb and Joe Jackson are the only players in this century to post .400 batting averages and not win a batting title. When Jackson hit .408 in 1911, Cobb batted .420 to beat him.

1.7   C. The Yankees were evicted from their home park

From 1913 to 1922, the New York Giants shared the Polo Grounds with the Yankees. The arrangement suited the Giants, who consistently outdrew their AL tenants. But when the Yankees acquired Babe Ruth in 1920, the dynamics of the relationship changed. That year, the Yankees set a new major-league attendance record, drawing 1,289,422 spectators, 360,000 more than the Giants. When the Giants' attendance fell even further behind that of the Yankees in 1921, owner Charles Stoneham served an eviction notice on his upstart tenants. Said Giants manager John McGraw: "If we kick

Ty Cobb: He played every game as if it were his last.

them out, they won't be able to find another location on Manhattan Island. They'll have to move to the Bronx or Long Island. The fans will forget them and they'll be through." The Yankees built their stadium in the Bronx, just across the Harlem River from the Polo Grounds. The huge ballpark, which had a seating capacity of 62,000, some 20,000 more than the Polo Grounds, opened in 1923. Although the Yankees drew fewer fans in their first season at Yankee Stadium than they had in the previous three years at the Polo Grounds, McGraw's prediction proved woefully inaccurate. With Ruth leading the way, the Yankees and their fabulous new stadium became the epitome of baseball glamor.

YANKEES–GIANTS ANNUAL ATTENDANCE (1919–1924)

Year	Yankees	AL Finish	Giants	NL Finish
1919	619,164	Third	708,857	Second
1920	1,289,422	Third	929,609	Second
1921	1,230,696	First	773,477	First
1922	1,026,134	First	945,809	First
1923	1,007,066	First	820,780	First
1924	1,053,533	Second	844,068	First

1.8 **A. 1921**
On July 6, 1921, Ruth blasted the 137th homer of his career to depose Roger Connor as baseball's all-time clout king. Connor, who played 18 seasons between 1880 and 1897, hit his 136 homers in 1,998 games. When Ruth passed Connor, he had been an everyday player for less than three years. Each of the next 577 homers Ruth hit merely extended his own record.

1.9 **D. Mickey Cochrane of the Tigers**
In 1933, the Detroit Tigers finished fifth, 25 games behind the AL-champion Washington Senators, so when Detroit jumped to first place in 1934, winning a franchise-record 101 games and capturing its first pennant since 1909, it was a major surprise. Several Bengals contributed to the team's dramatic improvement, but

none more so than hard-nosed catcher Mickey Cochrane, who had been purchased in the offseason from the Philadelphia Athletics for $100,000. "Cochrane was the spark that ignited us. He was our inspirational leader," said Hank Greenberg. In addition to handling catching duties, Cochrane also served as manager. Although his stats (.320 average, two homers, 76 RBI) looked puny in comparison with those of several other American Leaguers, most notably Triple Crown–winner Lou Gehrig, who hit .363 with 49 homers and 165 RBI, Cochrane got the nod from the voters as MVP, edging teammate Charlie Gehringer by two votes.

1.10 A. $1

In 1935, Cleveland Indians scout Cy Slapnicka journeyed to Iowa to check out reports about a 16-year-old pitcher named Bob Feller, who was said to possess an unholy fastball. After watching Feller pitch for the Farmers Union team of Des Moines, Slapnicka signed the teenager to a contract that would pay him $75 a month. Feller's signing bonus was $1 and a baseball autographed by the Indians. Slapnicka returned to Cleveland and informed his employers that he had found "the greatest pitcher in history." In 1936, Feller traveled with the team as a non-roster player. At an exhibition game during the All-Star break, the Indians let him pitch three innings against the world champion St. Louis Cardinals. The 17-year-old allowed just two hits and fanned *eight* Redbirds. After the game, umpire Red Ormsby, who had been around since 1923, pronounced Feller faster than Walter Johnson or Lefty Grove.

1.11 B. Gabby Hartnett of the Cubs

Midway through the 1938 season, the Cubs were in third place—six-and-half games behind the Pirates—when catcher Gabby Hartnett was appointed player-manager. The Cubs' play immediately improved, and they closed the gap. With a week to go, they were only one-and-a-half games back, as Pittsburgh came to town for a crucial three-game series. The Cubs won the first game 2–1 behind the pitching of Dizzy Dean. The next game was knotted 5–5 at the end of the eighth. Since daylight was fading fast and Wrigley Field had no lights, the umpires decided to allow only one more inning of play. If the game was still tied after the ninth, it would be replayed as part of a doubleheader the next day—a severe disadvantage to Chicago, because its pitching staff was exhausted. The Bucs went down in order in the top of the ninth. Pitching in a murky gloom, Pittsburgh's Mace Brown quickly disposed of the first two Chicago hitters in the bottom of the frame. Next up was Hartnett. Brown got two strikes on him, but then grooved a curve. The wily veteran ripped it over the left-field wall to give the Cubs a 6–5 victory. As he circled the bases, Hartnett was engulfed by jubilant teammates and fans. Remembered as "the homer in the gloamin'," the dramatic blow demoralized the Pirates, who bowed meekly the next day, 10–1. Having swept the series, the Cubs coasted to the pennant by two games.

1.12 C. Paul and Lloyd Waner

Although the hard-hitting Waners did have a toxic effect on opposition pitchers, a Dodger fan with a Brooklyn accent was reportedly responsible for giving them their nicknames. Bemoaning the frequent pastings the Waners gave Dodger pitchers, the fan said, "Every time you look up those Waner boys are on base; it's always the little poyson on third and the big poyson on first." With the NL-champion Pirates in 1927, Paul rapped 237 hits and Lloyd 223; their total of 460 hits set a single-season record for siblings. Between them, the Waners collected 5,611 career hits.

1.13 B. Philadelphia's Baker Bowl

Baker Bowl boasted several unusual features. During the 1920s, William Baker, the Phillies' spendthrift owner, used sheep to trim the infield and outfield grass. Cared for by the groundskeepers, the sheep had their own living quarters under the stands. The stadium also had a hump in the outfield where a railroad tunnel ran beneath the park. But its most celebrated feature was a 40-foot-high wall (raised to 60 feet in 1929) that extended from the center-field clubhouse to the right-field foul line. The wall was only 272 feet from home plate down the foul line and a mere 310 feet away in the right-center field power alley. Wrote sports columnist Red Smith: "It might be exaggerating to say that the outfield wall cast a shadow across the infield, but if the right fielder had eaten onions at lunch, the second baseman knew it." The cozy dimensions were tailor-made for portside-swinging Phillies. In 1929, Lefty O'Doul hit .453 at Baker Bowl as compared with .341 on the road. In 1930, Chuck Klein hit .443 at home and .329 elsewhere.

1.14 A. 40–7

It wasn't just the number of World Series the Yankees won during the era but the way they did it that earned them legendary status. In their ten Series triumphs between 1920 and 1945, the Yankees crushed their National League foes, winning 40 games and losing only seven, for a winning percentage of .851. In the seven Series the Yankees played in between 1927 and 1939, they won 28 games and lost three, outscoring their NL opponents 200 to 91.

1.15 B. Babe Dahlgren

Ironically, when Lou Gehrig left the Yankee lineup in 1939, he was replaced at first base by a Boston Red Sox castoff called Babe. However, nothing else about Ellsworth "Babe" Dahlgren resembled either Babe Ruth or Gehrig. The Yankees acquired Dahlgren in 1937 as a utility player, but Gehrig's sudden illness thrust him into a starting role. Dahlgren hit only .235 in 1939, but he did drive in 89 runs. He held the first-base job for two years, until Yankee management, irked by his contract demands, replaced him with Johnny Sturm.

1.16 C. Hank Greenberg in 1935

Since 1931, when the Baseball Writers Association of America assumed control of the MVP voting, only 13 of the 132 winners have been unanimous choices. Greenberg of the 1935 Detroit Tigers was the only MVP from the era to manage the feat. Some of his numbers were unspectacular (.328 batting average, 36 homers), but his RBI total was a shocker. Greenberg drove in 170 runs, a whopping 51 more than his closest rival, Lou Gehrig, with 119. This is by far the largest gap between a first- and second-place finisher in the RBI race. The next-highest margin in history was posted by the Cardinals' Joe Medwick, who bested runner-up Frank Demaree by 39 RBI in 1937. Greenberg was a terror with runners in scoring position in 1935. "You could see Hank really bearing down out there with men on base," noted teammate Charlie Gehringer. "He was always an intense hitter, but with men on base his concentration was really fierce." Incredibly, Greenberg did not make the All-Star team in 1935, even as a backup, although he had already amassed 110 RBI by the break. The first-base slots went to Lou Gehrig and Jimmie Foxx.

LARGEST MARGINS OF VICTORY BY RBI LEADERS*

Year	Team	Leader and Runner-up	RBI	Margin
1935	Tigers	Hank Greenberg	170	51
	Yankees	Lou Gehrig	119	
1937	Cardinals	Joe Medwick	154	39
	Cubs	Frank Demaree	115	
1913	Athletics	Frank Baker	126	36
	Athletics	Stuffy McInnis	90	
1910	Phillies	Sherry Magee	123	35
	Reds	Mike Mitchell	88	
1913	Phillies	Gavy Cravath	128	33
	Cubs	Heinie Zimmerman	95	
1921	Yankees	Babe Ruth	171	32
	Tigers	Harry Heilmann	139	

*CURRENT TO 1997

1.17 A. Lefty Gomez

The Yankee ace started five of the first six midsummer classics and was the winning pitcher in the American League's 4–2, 4–1 and 8–3 victories in 1933, 1935 and 1937. Although a notoriously poor hitter, Gomez also drove in the first run in All-Star game history. A renowned money pitcher, he also won six of the seven World Series games he started without suffering a defeat.

1.18 A. 1,000

The St. Louis Browns were never a very successful franchise, either at the gate or on the field, but their attendance really suffered when the Cardinals, with whom they shared Sportsman's Park, surged to the top of the National League in 1926. The

Cards remained a power for most of the 1930s, while the Browns wallowed in the American League's second division. For 18 straight years, from 1926 to 1943, the Browns had the worst attendance in baseball. In 1935, they drew only 80,922 fans in 77 home dates, an average of about 1,000 paid admissions per game.

1.19 A. Pete Gray of the Browns

With more than 200 big leaguers in the military during World War II, many marginal players found employment in the majors. None was more controversial than outfielder Pete Gray, who had only one arm, having lost his right limb in a childhood mishap. Based on his 1944 MVP performance with the Memphis Chicks of the Southern Association, where he batted .333 and stole 68 bases, Gray deserved a shot at the big time. However, during his stint with the St. Louis Browns in 1945, the 30-year-old rookie proved to be overmatched. Gray had little power, and since he compensated for his disability by starting his swing early, pitchers soon realized he had trouble with changeups. In the outfield, he had to remove his glove from his hand before making a throw, allowing runners to take liberties on the basepaths. Although Gray was a fan favourite, some of his teammates resented his presence, believing that his play was hurting the team's chances of repeating as AL champions. After hitting .218 in 77 games, Gray was returned to the minors.

1.20 D. Frankie Frisch

A fiery leader and superb defensive player, Frisch held the record for most World Series games (50) until 1951, when Joe DiMaggio passed him by playing his 51st and final postseason game. The flashy infielder appeared in eight Fall Classics—four with the Giants and four with the Cardinals—the last one in the role of player-manager. Frisch still holds the mark for most World Series games played by a National Leaguer, as well as the all-time Series record for doubles with ten.

GAME 4

WHAT'S MY LINE?

When asked prior to the 1934 season to assess the chances of the Brooklyn Dodgers, New York Giants manager Bill Terry replied, "Brooklyn! Is Brooklyn still in the league?" Those words would come back to haunt Terry. After leading the National League for most of the 1934 season, the Giants entered the final weekend tied for first with the hard-charging St. Louis Cardinals. As fate would have it, Terry's club hosted the sixth-place Dodgers in the last two games. Brooklyn dealt its bitter rival a death blow, beating the Giants 5–1 and 8–5, while the Cardinals swept the Cincinnati Reds to claim the pennant. The object of this game is to match the baseball personalities listed below with their memorable quotes. *(Answers are on page 139)*

Ty Cobb   Lou Gehrig   Babe Ruth   Satchel Paige
Mel Ott   Dizzy Dean   Lefty Gomez   Rogers Hornsby
John McGraw   Babe Herman   Casey Stengel   Eddie Cicotte
Leo Durocher   Ted Williams   Branch Rickey   Rabbit Maranville

1. "I have played a crooked game and I have lost."

2. "The good Lord was good to me. He gave me a strong body, a good right arm and weak mind."

3. "Good pitching will always stop good hitting and vice-versa."

4. "I have only one superstition. I make sure I touch all the bases when I hit a home run."

5. "Every time I sign a ball, and there must have been thousands, I thank my luck that I wasn't born Coveleski or Wambsganss or Peckinpaugh."

6. "The ballplayer who loses his head, who can't keep his cool, is worse than no ballplayer at all."

7. "Be in a hurry to win. Don't be in a hurry to lose."

8. "Age is a question of mind over matter. If you don't mind, it doesn't matter."

9. "Show me a good loser, and I'll show you an idiot."

10. "I'd rather be lucky than good."

11. "Never once did I get hit on the head by a fly ball. Once or twice on the shoulder maybe, but never on the head."

12. "I'll kill anyone that gets in my way."

13. "Baseball is the only endeavor where a man can succeed three times out of ten and and be considered a good performer."

14. "There is much less drinking now than there was before 1927, because I quit drinking on May 24, 1927."

15. "Luck is the residue of design."

16. "Don't read, it'll hurt your eyes."

Jimmie Foxx:
They're still
waiting for some
of the balls he hit
to come down.

Chapter Two

THE GUNS OF SUMMER

Baseball changed radically in the 1920s. The impact of Babe Ruth, the advent of smaller parks, the introduction of a livelier ball and the banning of the spitball and other trick pitches all helped spark a batting boom. The cannon fire reached its crescendo in 1930. That year the *entire* National League combined to bat a resounding .303. Three NL players—Bill Terry, Chuck Klein and Babe Herman—had more than 240 hits, while Hack Wilson blasted 56 homers and an all-time record 190 RBI. In the American League, RBI leader Lou Gehrig drove in a mere 174. The fans loved the offensive fireworks. Attendance topped the ten million mark in 1930, the most of any season between 1901 and 1945. It was a good time to be anyone but a pitcher. *(Answers are on page 25)*

2.1 **In 1920, Babe Ruth stunned baseball observers by blasting 54 homers. How large a margin did Ruth enjoy over his closest rival in the home-run race?**

A. 20 homers

B. 25 homers

C. 30 homers

D. 35 homers

2.2 **Who said, "All I want out of life is that when I walk down the street, folks will say, 'There goes the greatest hitter that ever lived' "?**

A. Ty Cobb

B. Babe Ruth

C. Ted Williams

D. Rogers Hornsby

2.3 **Who is the only player to hit 30 homers or more in 12 straight seasons?**

A. Babe Ruth

B. Mel Ott

C. Jimmie Foxx

D. Joe DiMaggio

2.4 **Al Simmons owns the record for the most consecutive 100-RBI seasons from the start of a career. How many straight years did Simmons top the century mark?**

A. Five

B. Eight

C. 11

D. 14

2.5 **Who is the only player to rip six hits and three homers in one game?**

A. Ty Cobb

B. Lou Gehrig

C. Bill Terry

D. Stan Musial

2.6 **Which duo owns the National League record for most combined homers in a season?**

A. The Giants' Mel Ott and Johnny Mize

B. The Cardinals' Joe Medwick and Rip Collins

C. The Cubs' Hack Wilson and Gabby Hartnett

D. The Phillies' Chuck Klein and Lefty O'Doul

2.7   In 1927, Babe Ruth slammed 60 round-trippers. In which month of that record-breaking season did Ruth hit the most homers?
A. May
B. June
C. August
D. September

2.8   Who made a serious run at breaking Babe Ruth's mark of 60 homers in 1938, reaching 58 homers with five games left to play in the season?
A. Mel Ott
B. Lou Gehrig
C. Jimmie Foxx
D. Hank Greenberg

2.9   How many hits did Ted Williams get on the last day of the 1941 season, when he batted .406?
A. None
B. Two
C. Four
D. Six

2.10   What was Joe DiMaggio's batting average during his fabled 56-game hitting streak in 1941?
A. .358
B. .408
C. .458
D. .508

2.11   Which American Leaguer captured four batting titles during the 1920s?
A. Ty Cobb
B. Tris Speaker
C. George Sisler
D. Harry Heilmann

2.12 **Who was traded a month after he won the Triple Crown?**
A. Joe Medwick
B. Chuck Klein
C. Jimmie Foxx
D. Rogers Hornsby

2.13 **Who collected a record 12 RBI in a game against the Brooklyn Dodgers on September 16, 1924?**
A. Pie Traynor of the Pirates
B. Jim Bottomley of the Cardinals
C. Cy Williams of the Phillies
D. Edd Roush of the Reds

2.14 **Who was the only player from the era to hit 30 homers and steal 30 bases in the same season?**
A. Ken Williams of the Browns
B. Bob Meusel of the Yankees
C. Kiki Cuyler of the Cubs
D. Pete Reiser of the Dodgers

2.15 **Who became the youngest player in history to hit 40 homers in a season, when he stroked 42 at age 20?**
A. Mel Ott
B. Hal Trosky
C. Jimmie Foxx
D. Joe DiMaggio

2.16 **Which shortstop hit .388 in 1936, an all-time high for his position?**
A. Luke Appling of the White Sox
B. Joe Cronin of the Red Sox
C. Arky Vaughan of the Pirates
D. Travis Jackson of the Giants

Answers

THE GUNS OF SUMMER

2.1   **D. 35 homers**

Ruth dialed long distance 54 times with the Yankees in 1920, an outrageous number by the standards of the day. His closest rival was the Browns' George Sisler, who hit 19 homers. The National League leader was the Phillies' Cy Williams, with 15. Ruth's homer output not only exceeded his career total (49) prior to that year, it was more homers than all but one other team managed to hit. Only the Phillies, with 64, topped him.

2.2   **C. Ted Williams**

Williams clearly didn't want for confidence, although he was often lacking in social graces. Cocky, petulant and self-absorbed, the 19-year-old alienated many people when he arrived for his first spring training with the Red Sox in 1938. He called star pitcher Lefty Grove "a funny-looking geezer," addressed manager Joe Cronin as "sport" and assured owner Tom Yawkey, "Don't look so worried, Tom. [Jimmie] Foxx and I will take care of everything." Williams did not make the big club that spring and was assigned to the Minneapolis Millers of the American Association. Red Sox outfielders Joe Vosmik, Doc Cramer and Ben Chapman jeered his departure with remarks like "good-bye busher." Williams sent them a message through clubhouse attendant Johnny Orlando: "Tell 'em I'll be back and tell them I'm going to wind up making more money in this friggin' game than the three of them put together." As was the case with most of his boasts, Williams made good on this one too.

2.3 C. Jimmie Foxx

Few could rival the awesome power of this brawny Maryland farm boy, who cut off his shirt sleeves to display his massive biceps. "Even his hair has muscles," an opposing pitcher complained. Baseballs flew off Foxx's bat like heat-seeking missiles. He once hit a ball with such force that it smashed a seat in the upper corner of the third deck of Yankee Stadium. Foxx belted 30 homers or more in 12 consecutive seasons from 1929 to 1940, a feat no other big leaguer has matched. In 1932, with the Philadelphia Athletics, Foxx hit 58 homers and would likely have broken Babe Ruth's record of 60 if he had not hurt his wrist falling off a stepladder in September.

2.4 C. 11

Al Simmons played baseball with a terrifying intensity. "I was a fighting, snarling animal on the field and I am proud, not ashamed of that reputation," he once said. Simmons joined the Philadelphia Athletics in 1924 and immediately proved he belonged, batting .308 with 102 RBI. But the young outfielder was just getting warmed up. The next year he batted .384, ripped 253 hits and amassed 129 RBI. Simmons would drive in more than 100 runs in each of his first 11 seasons, a feat unequaled in big-league annals.

2.5 A. Ty Cobb

Cobb always claimed he could have hit homers with the best of them if he had altered his batting stroke and swung for the fences. To prove his point, prior to a game against the St. Louis Browns on May 5, 1925, he told reporters, "Gentleman, pay close attention today. I'll show you something new. For the first time in my career I'll deliberately be going for home runs." In six at-bats, Cobb ripped three homers, a double and two singles, in a 14–8 rout of the Browns. That gave him an AL-record 16 total bases on the day. Cobb renewed his assault the next day, slamming another pair of four-baggers. Two other long drives were caught at the wall. Cobb's feat of five homers in two days has never been surpassed, nor has his mark of 25 total bases in two successive games. It was remarkable display, especially considering the Georgia Peach was a ripe old 38 at the time.

2.6 **C. The Cubs' Hack Wilson and Gabby Hartnett**

The Chicago Cubs belted 171 homers in 1930, with much of the thunder being supplied by outfielder Hack Wilson and catcher Gabby Hartnett. Wilson blasted 56 out of the park, while Hartnett went deep 37 times. Although their total of 93 homers is far short of the record 115 round-trippers hit by Roger Maris and Mickey Mantle in 1961, it is the most by any duo in NL history.

MOST HOMERS BY A NATIONAL LEAGUE DUO*

Year	Team	Players	HR	Total
1930	Cubs	Hack Wilson	56	93
		Gabby Hartnett	37	
1965	Giants	Willie Mays	52	91
		Willie McCovey	39	
1997	Rockies	Larry Walker	49	90
		Andres Galarraga	41	
1947	Giants	Johnny Mize	51	87
		Willard Marshall	36	
1955	Reds	Ted Kluszewski	47	87
		Wally Post	40	
1996	Rockies	Andres Galarraga	47	87
		Ellis Burks	40	
		Vinny Castilla	40	

*CURRENT TO 1997

2.7 **D. September**

For much of the 1927 season, the AL home-run derby was a duel between Babe Ruth and Lou Gehrig. On August 10, the 24-year-old Gehrig led the legend, 38 homers to 35, and many were convinced that Ruth's reign as baseball's home-run king was over. But Gehrig's emergence as a long-ball threat proved advantageous to Ruth. With Gehrig hitting behind him in the batting order, Ruth suddenly began seeing more hittable pitches than he had in years, and he responded with a late-season surge, belting 25 homers in his last 42 games, his pace becoming faster as the season wound down. In contrast, Gehrig faded down the stretch, hitting only nine homers after August 10. Ruth clubbed 17 homers in September, an all-time record for the month, including seven in his last nine games. On September 30, in the second-last game of the season, he hit number 60 at Yankee Stadium. After the game, Ruth whooped it up in the clubhouse, shouting, "Sixty, count 'em, sixty! Let's see some other son-of-a-bitch match that!"

2.8   D. Hank Greenberg

Late in the summer of 1938, the country's attention began to focus on Greenberg's pursuit of Babe Ruth's record of 60 homers. On August 31, the Tigers' slugger poled his 46th dinger, putting him six games ahead of Ruth's 1927 pace. Asked if he thought he could break Ruth's mark, Greenberg replied, "I've heard that question so much that I even hear it in my sleep." In addition to the pressure of pursuing Ruth's hallowed record, the Jewish first baseman also had to contend with racial epithets from fans and players. On September 27, Greenberg clubbed homers number 57 and 58 during a doubleheader with the Browns, which left him two shy of Ruth's record with five games to go. Then, his bat went cold. He entered the season's finale—a doubleheader versus the Indians at cavernous Municipal Stadium—stalled at 58. His pitching opponent in the first game was 19-year-old Bob Feller, who stole the show, fanning 18 Tigers to set a new single-game strikeout record. In four at-bats, Greenberg managed a 450-foot double off the fence in left-center, a home run in most parks. He rapped three singles in three trips to the plate in the second game, which was called after seven innings because of darkness. Time and daylight ran out on Greenberg at the same time.

2.9   D. Six

Ted Williams entered the last day of the 1941 season with a .39955 batting average, which rounds off to .400. With the pennant race decided, Boston manager Joe Cronin suggested that Williams sit out the Red Sox's doubleheader against the Athletics to preserve his .400 average. Williams replied: "I don't care to be known as a .400 hitter with a lousy average of .39955. I'm going to be a .400 hitter." In the first game, he ripped a homer and three singles in five at-bats. In the nightcap, he collected a double and a single in three

Hank Greenberg: He chased Babe Ruth's homer record in 1938.

at-bats. With his six hits on the day, the Splendid Splinter finished the year at .406 to become the AL's first .400 hitter since Harry Heilmann in 1923. Interestingly, the sacrifice-fly rule was not in effect in 1941. Had it been, Williams—who drove home at least a dozen runners on fly balls during the season—would not have needed to perform his last-day heroics in order to hit .400. He would have easily surpassed the mark.

2.10 B. .408

Consistency was the hallmark of Joe DiMaggio, so it is ironic that he is best remembered for a hitting streak. Unlike some individual hitting records, this one had a big impact on the pennant race. The Yankees were 14–14 when it started, but were 55–27 and solidly in first place when it ended. During his 56-game hitting streak, DiMaggio also scored 56 runs and had 56 hits. After the streak was snapped, DiMaggio began another one, hitting safely in 16 straight games, giving him a hit in 72 of 73 games. During his 56-game run, DiMaggio batted .408.

2.11 D. Harry Heilmann

Heilmann was an odd player. The Tiger outfielder won four batting titles during the 1920s, but only in odd years. Heilmann bested teammate Ty Cobb .394 to .389 in 1921, and he topped Babe Ruth .403 to .393 in 1923. In 1925, he passed Tris Speaker with a couple of games left in the season and won .393 to .389. In 1927, he nipped Al Simmons .398 to .392. Four batting titles with averages of .403, .398, .394 and .393—not too shabby. If Heilmann had managed one more hit in 1927 and four more in 1921 and 1925, he would have batted .400 four times and his name would be much more familiar today.

2.12 B. Chuck Klein

The Philadelphia Phillies' right fielder was one of the NL's most feared hitters, reaching the 200-hit plateau in each of his first five full seasons and topping the loop in homers four times. But after Klein won the Triple Crown in 1933, the cash-strapped Phillies dealt him to the Cubs for three players and $65,000. Soon after, his career took a rapid downturn. Some say it was caused by leaving the cozy confines of Baker Bowl, a park that favored lefty hitters. Yet when Klein was traded back to the Phils in 1936, he failed to display his former explosiveness with the bat. According to the Cubs' Billy Herman, Klein destroyed himself by attempting to play through a leg injury. "Klein got off to a great start with us, but then he pulled a hamstring muscle. He was a hell of a competitor, but he was just tearing up that leg. The blood started to clot in it, and I swear, that leg turned black, from his left thigh all the way down to his ankle. I think it just about ruined his career. He couldn't run anymore, he couldn't swing anymore." Klein, who had a career average of .359 to this point, averaged only .278 for the rest of his career and never again hit 30 homers in a season. After batting .218 in 1940, at age 35, Klein was through as an everyday player, a sad finish to what had been a brilliant beginning.

CHUCK KLEIN'S TWO-SIDED CAREER

	G	AB	R	H	2B	3B	HR	RBI	AVE
1928–1933	823	3,367	699	1,209	246	50	191	757	.359
1934–1944	930	3,119	469	867	152	24	109	544	.278

2.13 B. Jim Bottomley of the Cardinals

Bottomley gave new meaning to the term cleanup hitter, when he drove in a record 12 runs against five Brooklyn pitchers in a 17–3 Cardinals rampage at Ebbets Field on September 16, 1924. Bottomley delivered his first two runs with a first-inning single off Rube Erhardt. In the second, he doubled home a run off Bonnie Hollingsworth. In the fourth, he clubbed a grand slam off Art Decatur, upping his RBI total to seven. In the sixth, he rocked Decatur for a two-run homer. In the seventh, Bottomley singled home two runners against Tex Wilson to raise his ribbie total to 11. In the ninth, he made it an even dozen, singling off Jim Roberts to drive home a runner from third base, to cap a 6-for-6 day and break the single-game mark of 11 RBI, set in 1892. Ironically, the man who held the former record was Wilbert Robinson, Brooklyn's manager that day. Robinson showed a lot of class in letting his staff pitch to Bottomley even as the Redbirds' slugger was demolishing his cherished mark. A lesser man might have ordered his pitchers to give Bottomley a couple of intentional passes.

2.14 A. Ken Williams of the Browns

Players who combined base-stealing speed and home-run power were rare in baseball's earlier days. Williams was an exception. With Babe Ruth sidelined for a large chunk of the 1922 season with various suspensions, the Browns' outfielder won the AL home-run title with 39 circuit blasts. He also stole 47 bases, for a combined total of 86 homers and steals. The majors would not see another 30–30 man until Willie Mays joined the club in 1956.

2.15 A. Mel Ott

In 1929, Chuck Klein of the Philadelphia Phillies hit 43 homers to break Rogers Hornsby's NL record of 42. But an even bigger story was the performance of Mel Ott of the New York Giants, who poled 42 dingers and 151 RBI at age 20. No player so young has ever hit so many homers or driven in so many runs. Ott, a catcher in the semipro ranks, joined the Giants in 1926, at age 17. A lefty hitter, Ott raised his front leg up to knee level as the pitcher was in his motion and then stepped into his swing. Because of Ott's unorthodox batting style, manager John McGraw refused to send him to the minors for fear that someone would tamper with his swing. For two years, McGraw used his young protégé mostly as a pinch-hitter, while teaching him the finer points of playing the outfield. Dubbed "the Boy Bomber" by New York writers when he became a regular at age 19, Ott played 22 seasons in the Big Apple, clouting 511 career homers.

2.16 A. Luke Appling of the White Sox

Appling was known as "Old Aches and Pains" because he was constantly griping about his physical miseries. Yet, despite his nickname he suffered only one serious injury in his 15-year career—a broken ankle in 1938. A slap-hitting, bat-control artist, Appling would deliberately foul off pitches until he got one he liked. In 1936, he hit .388, the highest average ever posted by a shortstop. It also marked the first time a White Sox player had won a batting title. Appling snared a second batting crown with the Pale Hose in 1943.

DIAMOND MONIKERS

During the 1920s and 1930s, baseball was rich with distinctive nicknames. Match each of these players with his diamond moniker.

(Answers are on page 139)

1.	_____	Jimmie Foxx	A. "The Iron Horse"
2.	_____	Rogers Hornsby	B. "Ducky"
3.	_____	Joe Medwick	C. "The Meal Ticket"
4.	_____	Mel Ott	D. "Memphis"
5.	_____	Lou Gehrig	E. "Country"
6.	_____	Tommy Henrich	F. "The Boy Bomber"
7.	_____	Ernie Lombardi	G. "The Fordham Flash"
8.	_____	Frankie Frisch	H. "Rajah"
9.	_____	Bill Terry	I. "Schnozz"
10.	_____	Marty Marion	J. "Old Reliable"
11.	_____	Carl Hubbell	K. "The Beast"
12.	_____	Enos Slaughter	L. "The Octopus"

Dizzy Dean:
Brash, funny,
often quotable
and always
tough to beat.

Chapter Three

KINGS OF THE HILL

Dizzy Dean once declared: "Anybody who's ever had the privilege of seein' me play ball knows that I am the greatest pitcher in the world." Some might dispute that claim, but there is no denying that the former Arkansas cotton picker was a superb showman. His infectious optimism and cornpone wit, coupled with a crackling fastball, made him a huge attraction during the bleak Depression years. Dean called himself "the Great One" and made bold predictions. Prior to the 1934 season, he forecast that he and his brother Paul, a 20-year-old rookie, would win 45 games and lead the Cardinals to the pennant. Dizzy won 30, Paul won 19, and St. Louis took the flag. Before the 1934 World Series against the Detroit Tigers, Dizzy boasted, "Me and Paul are gonna win four." The Deans delivered and the Redbirds were kings of the hill. *(Answers are on page 39)*

3.1 **Which pitcher led the National League in strikeouts seven straight years from 1922 to 1928?**

A. Dazzy Vance

B. Eppa Rixey

C. Burleigh Grimes

D. Grover Alexander

3.2 **Who made history by tossing back-to-back no-hitters in 1938?**
A. Bob Feller of the Indians
B. Red Ruffing of the Yankees
C. Tex Carleton of the Cubs
D. Johnny Vander Meer of the Reds

3.3 **New York Giants hurler Carl Hubbell owns the major-league record for most consecutive wins. How many victories in a row did Hubbell chalk up without a defeat?**
A. 18
B. 21
C. 24
D. 27

3.4 **Who compiled a 50–6 won–lost record as a starting pitcher in back-to-back seasons?**
A. Dizzy Dean of the Cardinals
B. Lefty Grove of the Athletics
C. Bob Feller of the Indians
D. Carl Hubbell of the Giants

3.5 **Which pitcher was known as "Ol' Stubblebeard"?**
A. Urban Shocker
B. Stan Coveleski
C. Grover Alexander
D. Burleigh Grimes

3.6 **How often did Bob Feller allow one hit or less in a game?**
A. Never
B. Five times
C. Ten times
D. 15 times

3.7 **Who led the majors in complete games and saves in 1936?**
A. Wes Ferrell of the Red Sox
B. Schoolboy Rowe of the Tigers
C. Dizzy Dean of the Cardinals
D. Carl Hubbell of the Giants

3.8 Who posted a 15–1 record in 1937, to establish an AL-record winning percentage of .938?

A. Johnny Allen of the Indians

B. Lefty Gomez of the Yankees

C. Tommy Bridges of the Tigers

D. Monte Stratton of the White Sox

3.9 Which pitching duo combined to win the most games in a season during the era?

A. Jim Bagby and Stan Coveleski of the 1920 Indians

B. Lefty Grove and George Earnshaw of the 1931 Athletics

C. Bucky Walters and Paul Derringer of the 1939 Reds

D. Hal Newhouser and Dizzy Trout of the 1944 Tigers

3.10 On August 10, 1944, Red Barrett of the Boston Braves registered a pitching first. What did Barrett do?

A. He allowed five homers in one inning

B. He struck out eight batters in a row

C. He pitched for two different teams in one day

D. He tossed a record-low 58 pitches in a complete-game shutout

3.11 What unusual pitching accomplishment do Bobo Newsom and Ray Kremer share?

A. Both tossed a 20-inning complete game

B. Both pitched no-hitters, but still lost the game

C. Both posted 20-win seasons with an ERA above 5.00

D. They are the only 200-game winners with losing records

3.12 What was Carl Hubbell's signature pitch?

A. The sinker

B. The slider

C. The screwball

D. The knuckleball

3.13 **Which 1940s moundsman made famous the "eephus" pitch?**
A. Rip Sewell of the Pirates
B. Max Lanier of the Cardinals
C. Spud Chandler of the Yankees
D. Dizzy Trout of the Tigers

3.14 **Which rookie tossed a perfect game against the hard-hitting Detroit Tigers on April 30, 1922?**
A. George Uhle of the Indians
B. Jim Brillheart of the Senators
C. Gus Ketchum of the Athletics
D. Charlie Robertson of the White Sox

3.15 **Who is the only pitcher to win back-to-back MVP awards?**
A. Bob Feller of the Indians
B. Hal Newhouser of the Tigers
C. Carl Hubbell of the Giants
D. Lefty Grove of the Athletics

3.16 **Who owns the best career-winning percentage of any pitcher with more than 100 wins?**
A. Dizzy Dean
B. Lefty Grove
C. Spud Chandler
D. Babe Ruth

3.17 **In 1925, who became the first major leaguer to lead his league in games pitched without making a single start?**
A. Dixie Davis of the Browns
B. Firpo Marberry of the Senators
C. Jimmy Ring of the Phillies
D. Virgil Barnes of the Giants

KINGS OF THE HILL

3.1 **A. Dazzy Vance**

Vance had a curious career. Although he won 197 games, he did not post his first victory until age 31. Vance's problem was that he was not effective when pitching after only three days' rest—he needed four. He spent ten years in the minors before he found a manager who recognized the problem—Wilbert Robinson of the Dodgers. Under Robinson's regimen of four days' rest between starts, Vance became the NL's most dominating pitcher, topping the circuit in strikeouts seven straight seasons from 1922 to 1928. In 1924, the Brooklyn ace was 28–6 with 262 Ks, an astounding number considering that only one other NL pitcher fanned more than 86 that year.

3.2 **D. Johnny Vander Meer of the Reds**

On June 11, 1938, Vander Meer tossed a no-hitter versus the Boston Braves, winning 3–0. Four days later, the hard-throwing southpaw faced the Brooklyn Dodgers in the first night game at Ebbets Field. A crowd of 38,748, including Vander Meer's parents and 500 fans from his hometown of Prospect Park, New Jersey, attended the historic event. Vander Meer pitched brilliantly, holding the Dodgers hitless for eight innings as the Reds surged to a 6–0 lead. Then, in the ninth, his control suddenly vanished. After retiring Buddy Hassett on a grounder, he walked Babe Phelps, Cookie Lavagetto and Dolf Camilli to load the bases. But after a chat with manager Bill McKechnie, Vander Meer settled down. He retired Ernie Koy on a force at home, leaving only Leo Durocher to retire for his second straight no-no. Durocher stroked a soft fly to center fielder

Harry Craft, and Vander Meer joined the ranks of the immortals. The Dutch Master tossed three more hitless innings in his next game against Boston before Debs Garms singled, halting the hitless string at 21 innings. That left Vander Meer three shy of the record for consecutive hitless innings, set by Cy Young in 1904.

3.3   **C. 24**

From 1933 to 1937, Carl Hubbell had a run of five years in which he etched his name among the greatest pitchers of all time. During that span, the poker-faced southpaw led the NL in wins and ERA three times and posted won–lost records of 23–12, 21–12, 23–12, 26–6 and 22–8. Hubbell's mastery reached its peak during the last three months of 1936, when he logged 16 straight victories. He continued his string at the start of 1937, reeling off eight more consecutive wins. The 24-game winning streak finally ended on May 31, when the Giants' ace was knocked out of the box by the Dodgers in the third inning of a 10–3 rout.

3.4   **B. Lefty Grove of the Athletics**

Unlike most speedballers, Grove's fastball had no hop or sail to it. Even so, most hitters couldn't touch it. "It looked," said one batter, "like a piece of white sewing thread coming up at you." In 1930 and 1931, Grove was nearly unbeatable. In 62 starts, he posted a won–lost record of 50–6, for an incredible winning percentage of .893. He also won nine and lost three in relief. Grove's composite record for the two years was 59–9 with a 2.30 ERA. Even more amazing, he accomplished this at the height of the hitting era, when the ball was lively as a jackrabbit.

3.5   **D. Burleigh Grimes**

A notorious spitball artist, Grimes would chew slippery elm to increase his saliva production and make it easier to load up the ball. However, because the slippery elm irritated his skin, Grimes never shaved on the days he pitched. Since he always sported stubbly whiskers on the mound, players called him "Ol' Stubblebeard." The nickname suited Grimes's bellicose personality. Brushback pitches were a staple of his repertoire. "He made Bob Gibson and Don Drysdale look like the angels of mercy,"

Lefty Grove: "He could throw a lamb chop past a wolf."

said shortstop Dick Bartell, a teammate of Grimes in the late 1920s. "Ol' Stubblebeard" lost none of his nastiness as he aged. In 1934, Goose Goslin of the Tigers hit a homer off Grimes. Later in the game, as Goslin waited in the on-deck circle for his next at-bat, Grimes threw at him.

3.6   D. 15 times

It's a fine line between a no-hitter and a one-hitter—a bloop single, a seeing-eye grounder or a bunt can all spoil perfection. Bob Feller walked that fine line 15 times. On three occasions he twirled no-hitters; in the other 12 outings he allowed one hit. That's by far the most one-hit games in history. When Feller retired in 1956, he shared the record for most no-hitters (3) with Cy Young and Larry Corcoran. The total has since been surpassed by Nolan Ryan (7) and Sandy Koufax (4). But if Feller had not missed four prime years serving in World War II, or if he had a bit more luck in a few of his dozen one-hitters, he could be baseball's reigning no-hit king.

3.7   C. Dizzy Dean of the Cardinals

Dean earned his pay in 1936, making 51 appearances, pitching 315 innings and winning 24 games. He started 34 games, went the distance an NL-high 28 times and picked up a league-leading 11 saves. By topping the NL in complete games and saves, Dean managed a feat that had last been accomplished in 1910 by Three Finger Brown of the Cubs. Until scientists develop bionic arms, we can be sure it won't occur again.

3.8   A. Johnny Allen of the Indians

Allen came frustratingly close to compiling a flawless 16–0 mark in 1937. After notching 15 straight wins, the Indians hurler suffered his lone defeat in the season's last game, when he was beaten 1–0 by Jake Wade of the Tigers. Wade, who went on to register a lackluster 27–40 lifetime record, chose that day to turn in the best performance of his career, a one-hitter.

3.9   D. Hal Newhouser and Dizzy Trout of the 1944 Tigers

In a year when no other AL pitcher managed 20 wins, Newhouser won 29 and Trout 27, to account for 64 percent of Detroit's victories. Their combined win total (56) was the best of any pitching duo from the era. Yet, despite this formidable one-two punch, the Tigers failed to win the 1944 pennant, finishing one game behind the St. Louis Browns.

MOST WINS BY A PITCHING DUO (1920–1945)

Pitching Duo	Year	Team	W	L	Total
Hal Newhouser	1944	Tigers	29	9	56
Dizzy Trout			27	14	
Jim Bagby	1920	Indians	31	12	55
Stan Coveleski			24	14	
Lefty Grove	1931	Athletics	31	4	52
George Earnshaw			21	7	
Bucky Walters	1939	Reds	27	11	52
Paul Derringer			25	7	
Lefty Grove	1930	Athletics	28	5	50
George Earnshaw			22	13	
Dazzy Vance	1924	Dodgers	28	6	50
Burleigh Grimes			22	13	

3.10   **D. He tossed a record-low 58 pitches in a complete-game shutout**
On August 10, 1944, Red Barrett of the Boston Braves did the maximum with the minumum. He blanked the Cincinnati Reds 2–0 while throwing only 58 pitches—an average of about six pitches per inning, or two pitches per out. The contest took just 75 minutes to play, the shortest night game ever. Barrett's effort broke the previous record-low of 61 pitches, shared by Ben Sanders (1891) and Red Faber (1915).

3.11   **C. Both posted 20-win seasons with an ERA above 5.00**
Winning 20 games while allowing an average of more than five runs a game doesn't seem possible, but it happened twice during the hitting-happy 1930s. In 1930, Ray Kremer of the fifth-place Pittsburgh Pirates had a 20–12 record with a 5.02 ERA. In 1938, Bobo Newsom of the seventh-place St. Louis Browns was 20–15 with a 5.08 ERA.

Carl Hubbell: He was the NL MVP in 1933 and 1936.

3.12 C. The screwball

The screwball—also known as the fadeaway and the inshoot—breaks in the opposite direction of a curve ball. Several pitchers had used the pitch before Carl Hubbell, but no one threw it so often or so effectively as the Giants' ace. According to Hubbell, it wasn't so much the breaking action of his scroogie that fooled hitters, as the pitch's reduced speed. He threw it with the same arm motion as his fastball, so it worked like a changeup, confusing a batter's timing. "I faced that screwball many times," said Cincinnati's Frank McCormick, "and I can tell you exactly what the experience was like: there it was, and there it wasn't. You never took a more confident swing than the one you took at a Hubbell screwball, and you always walked back to the bench thinking the same thing: How the hell did that happen?"

3.13 **A. Rip Sewell of the Pirates**

Sewell had other pitches in his arsenal, but it was the eephus that made him famous. The pitch was given its name by Sewell's Pittsburgh Pirate teammate Maurice Van Robays, who said: "Eephus ain't no word, and that ain't no pitch." The pitch was lobbed in a high, blooping arc toward the plate. Batters found it difficult to hit, especially with any power. Sewell introduced the pitch in 1943, and for the first three years he used it no one came close to hitting it for a homer. Finally, at the 1946 All-Star game, Ted Williams drove one of Sewell's bloopers out of the park. It became one of the most celebrated homers in history.

3.14 **D. Charlie Robertson of the White Sox**

Robertson became the third hurler in the 20th century to toss a perfect game and the first to do it on the road, when he beat Detroit 2–0 on April 30, 1922, at Navin Field. Amazingly, Robertson pitched his no-hitter in only the third start of his career and against a Detroit team that batted .305 that year. No other pitcher has thrown a no-hitter against a team with such a potent lineup. The Tigers protested several times during the game that Robertson was using a spitter, and in the ninth inning, Ty Cobb, Detroit's player-manager, charged out of the dugout demanding that umpire Dick Nallin look at the ball. He not only inspected the ball, he examined the rookie's entire uniform. Apparently satisfied, Nallin let the game continue and Robertson retired the side in order.

3.15 **B. Hal Newhouser of the Tigers**

The Tiger lefty won the AL MVP award in 1944 and 1945. His record in 1944 was 29–9 with a 2.22 era and 187 strikeouts. In 1945, he was 25–9 with a 1.81 ERA and 212 strikeouts. Only teammate Dizzy Trout's 2.12 ERA in 1944 stopped him from topping the loop in all three categories in both seasons. Despite Newhouser's dominance, many dismissed his achievement as a wartime fluke. But that judgement seems unfair. Newhouser twice more led the AL in wins after 1945, and he fanned more batters than any other hurler during the 1940s. In fact, Newhouser nearly won a third straight MVP award in 1946, when he was 26–9 with a 1.94 ERA and 275 Ks. He lost by 27 votes to Ted Williams.

3.16 C. Spud Chandler

Chandler joined the Yankees in 1937, at age 29, but he didn't become a frontline starter until 1941, when he developed a wicked slider and suddenly became nearly unbeatable. From age 33 onward, his winning percentage was an incredible .740 and his ERA 2.33. In 1943, he went 20–4 and posted a 1.64 ERA, the lowest of any pitcher between 1920 and 1945. Chandler enlisted in the military in 1944 and served until the end of the war. He rejoined the Yanks in 1946, and even at 38, he was the team's best pitcher, going 20–8 with a 2.10 ERA. Chandler retired after the 1947 season with a .717 winning percentage, the best among pitchers with 100 or more victories.

HIGHEST WINNING PERCENTAGE (100 OR MORE WINS)*

Player	Career	W	L	Pct
Spud Chandler	1937–47	109	43	.717
Whitey Ford	1950–67	236	106	.690
Dave Foutz	1884–94	147	66	.690
Bob Caruthers	1884–92	218	99	.688
Don Gullett	1970–78	109	50	.686
Lefty Grove	1925–41	300	141	.680
Joe Wood	1908–20	116	57	.671
Vic Raschi	1946–55	132	66	.667
Christy Mathewson	1900–16	373	187	.665

*CURRENT TO 1997

3.17 B. Firpo Marberry of the Senators

Called Firpo because he resembled Luis Firpo, the Argentinian heavyweight boxer, Fred Marberry was the majors' first relief specialist. In 1925, with the Washington Senators, he became the first moundsman to lead his league in appearances (55) without making a single start. Later in his career, the rubber-armed righty also doubled as a starter. Until the 1960s, Marberry was the only pitcher with more than 100 career saves and more than 2,000 innings pitched.

T I M E   T R A V E L

Almost everyone remembers that Babe Ruth hit 60 homers in 1927 and that Ted Williams batted .406 in 1941. Pinning down other baseball landmarks requires more thought. The challenge here is to match the date with the event.   *(Answers are on page 139)*

1920	1922	1924	1928	1930	1933
1934	1935	1938	1939	1940	1941

1. _____ The first All-Star game is staged.

2. _____ John McGraw manages his last pennant winner.

3. _____ Ty Cobb collects his last hit.

4. _____ Hack Wilson drives in a ML-record 190 RBI.

5. _____ Babe Ruth plays his final game as a Yankee.

6. _____ The Negro National League is founded.

7. _____ Bob Feller tosses an opening-day no-hitter.

8. _____ The Baseball Hall of Fame opens its doors.

9. _____ Lefty Grove wins his 300th game.

10. _____ The first World Series radio broadcast is heard.

11. _____ The Cardinals trade Dizzy Dean to the Cubs.

12. _____ Night baseball makes its major-league debut.

Lou Gehrig:
He drove in 100
runs or more
in 13 straight
seasons.

Chapter Four

MAJOR-LEAGUE MILESTONES

Legend has it that Lou Gehrig's record consecutive-games streak began on June 2, 1925, when he replaced Yankees first baseman Wally Pipp, who had a headache. In fact, the streak started the day before, when Gehrig pinch-hit for shortstop Pee Wee Wanninger. Ironically, Wanninger had replaced Everett Scott, the player whose consecutive-games mark Gehrig would shatter in 1933. Before losing his job to Wanninger on May 5, 1925, Scott had played 1,307 straight games at shortstop. Pipp's replacement on the day he had a sore noggin was not Gehrig, but Fred Merkle, who gave way to Gehrig in the ninth inning. Larrupin' Lou's record lasted until 1995, when shortstop Cal Ripken, Jr. supplanted him as baseball's new iron man. *(Answers are on page 53)*

4.1 **Whose record 44-game hitting streak did Joe DiMaggio break in 1941, when he hit safely in 56 straight games?**

A. Ty Cobb's

B. Willie Keeler's

C. George Sisler's

D. Napoleon Lajoie's

4.2 **Who struck out Babe Ruth, Lou Gehrig, Jimmie Foxx, Al Simmons and Joe Cronin in succession at the 1934 All-Star game?**
A. Lon Warneke
B. Dizzy Dean
C. Carl Hubbell
D. Waite Hoyt

4.3 **What was significant about pitcher Burleigh Grimes's last major-league win on May 1, 1934?**
A. It gave him exactly 300 career wins
B. His son Oscar was the catcher that day
C. It made him the oldest pitcher in history to post a win
D. It was the last win by a pitcher who was legally permitted to throw a spitball

4.4 **Which rookie record did Ted Williams set in 1939?**
A. Most runs
B. Most hits
C. Most doubles
D. Most runs batted in

4.5 **In 1920, Babe Ruth posted the highest slugging average in major-league annals. What did he hit?**
A. .757
B. .787
C. .817
D. .847

4.6 **Who fanned just four times in 608 at-bats in 1925, the lowest ratio of strikeouts per at-bats in a season by an everyday player?**
A. Zack Wheat of the Dodgers
B. Pie Traynor of the Pirates
C. Joe Sewell of the Indians
D. Earle Combs of the Yankees

4.7 Which player once received five intentional walks in a single game?

A. Babe Ruth

B. Mel Ott

C. George Sisler

D. Ted Williams

4.8 Which ballpark was the site of the majors' first night game?

A. Chicago's Comiskey Park

B. Philadelphia's Shibe Park

C. Brooklyn's Ebbets Field

D. Cincinnati's Crosley Field

4.9 On May 1, 1920, Leon Cadore of the Brooklyn Dodgers and Joe Oeschger of the Boston Braves hooked up in the longest pitching duel in major-league history. How many innings did the two men pitch?

A. 20 innings

B. 23 innings

C. 26 innings

D. 29 innings

4.10 Who hit .353 in 1926, to become the first catcher to win a batting crown?

A. Earl Smith of the Pirates

B. Bubbles Hargrave of the Reds

C. Muddy Ruel of the Senators

D. Mickey Cochrane of the Athletics

4.11 Who is the only player to ever lead his league in homers and fewest strikeouts?

A. George Kelly of the 1921 Giants

B. Joe DiMaggio of the 1937 Yankees

C. Johnny Mize of the 1940 Cardinals

D. Tommy Holmes of the 1945 Braves

4.12 **What did Chuck Klein do in 1932 that has never been duplicated by another National League player?**
A. He twice hit for the cycle
B. He rapped five doubles in one game
C. He led the NL in homers and stolen bases
D. He made two unassisted double plays in the outfield

4.13 **Who is the only major leaguer to play every inning of seven straight All-Star games?**
A. Pie Traynor
B. Jimmie Foxx
C. Joe DiMaggio
D. Charlie Gehringer

4.14 **In what year was the first major-league game televised?**
A. 1936
B. 1939
C. 1942
D. 1945

4.15 **In 1932, Dale Alexander became the first player to do what?**
A. Pinch-hit for Babe Ruth
B. Hit two grand slams in one inning
C. Wear eyeglasses during a game
D. Win a batting title while playing for two teams

4.16 **Who was the first player to have his number retired?**
A. Ty Cobb
B. Tris Speaker
C. Babe Ruth
D. Lou Gehrig

Answers

MAJOR-LEAGUE MILESTONES

4.1 **B. Willie Keeler's**

On July 2, 1941, Joe DiMaggio homered off Red Sox pitcher Dick Newsome in an 8–4 Yankee win to eclipse Keeler's record 44-game hitting streak, set in 1897. After the game, in reference to Keeler's famous maxim "Keep your eye clear and hit 'em where they ain't," Yankee pitcher Lefty Gomez quipped, "Joe hit one today where they ain't." DiMaggio would extend his streak to 56 games before finally being held hitless by the Cleveland Indians.

LONGEST HITTING STREAKS*

Player	Year	Team	Games
Joe DiMaggio	1941	Yankees	56
Willie Keeler	1897	Orioles	44
Pete Rose	1978	Reds	44
Bill Dahlen	1894	Cubs	42
George Sisler	1922	Browns	41
Ty Cobb	1911	Tigers	40
Paul Molitor	1987	Brewers	39

* CURRENT TO 1997

4.2 **C. Carl Hubbell**

Hubbell got off to a rocky start at the 1934 All-Star game. The National League pitcher surrendered a leadoff single to Charlie Gehringer and a walk to Heinie Manush. Two men on, no outs and

53

Babe Ruth due up, followed by Lou Gehrig and Jimmie Foxx—not a promising scenario. Catcher Gabby Hartnett trotted out to confer with Hubbell. "We'll waste everything except the screwball. Get that over, but keep your fastball and hook outside. We can't let them hit in the air," said Hartnett. The advice proved invaluable. Artfully bending his scroogie over the outside corner, Hubbell proceeded to fan Ruth, Gehrig and Foxx. But he wasn't done yet. In the next inning, he struck out Al Simmons and Joe Cronin, before Bill Dickey finally slapped a single to left. That brought pitcher Lefty Gomez to the plate. Gomez turned to Hartnett and said, "You are now looking at a man whose career average is .104. What the hell am I doing up here?" Not much, as it turned out, because Gomez also went down on strikes. Hubbell's feat of fanning five of the game's greatest hitters in order remains one of baseball's most legendary episodes.

4.3 **D. It was the last win by a pitcher who was legally permitted to throw a spitball**

When baseball's arbiters outlawed the spitball and other trick pitches in 1920, they included a special clause that allowed each club to designate two pitchers as spitball pitchers. These hurlers were allowed to legally ply their salivary trade until the end of their careers. Grimes, the last of the breed, won his final game (the 270th of his career) in relief for the New York Yankees on May 1, 1934. It was certainly not the last win recorded by a pitcher who used a spitter, but it was the last time a hurler tossed the wet one with an umpire's blessing.

4.4 **D. Most runs batted in**

Ted Williams arrived in the majors with a bang in 1939, leading the American League with 145 RBI, which was 19 more than runner-up Joe DiMaggio. No one other freshman has ever driven in as many runs in a season, although Walt Dropo, who later played with Williams on the Red Sox, came close in 1950, knocking in 144. The rookie marks for most hits and most runs are both held by Lloyd Waner of the Pirates, who drilled 223 hits and scored 133 times in 1927. The rookie record for doubles belongs to Johnny Frederick, who smacked 52 for the Dodgers in 1929.

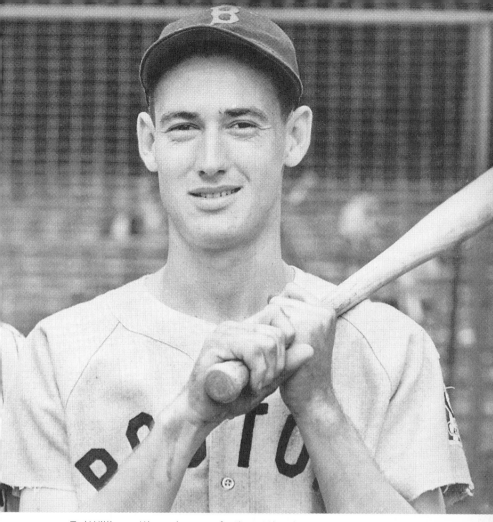

Ted Williams: His goal was perfection at the plate.

4.5   **D. .847**

Slugging average, which measures a hitter's power, is calculated by dividing a player's total bases by his at-bats. Babe Ruth is the only player to post a single-season slugging average above .800—and he did it twice, hitting a thunderous .847 in 1920, and an equally loud .846 in 1921. In fact, the Wazir of Wham owns four of the best five slugging averages of all time. Although Ruth's 1921 slugging average ranks second to his 1920 total by one percentage point, 1921 was arguably his greatest hitting year. The Yankee slugger compiled

177 runs, 204 hits, 44 doubles, 16 triples, 59 homers and 171 RBI. Mind-boggling as those numbers are, they would have been even higher if gun-shy AL pitchers had not walked Ruth 144 times.

THE BEST SINGLE-SEASON SLUGGING AVERAGES*

Player	Year	Team	Ave
Babe Ruth	1920	Yankees	.847
Babe Ruth	1921	Yankees	.846
Babe Ruth	1927	Yankees	.772
Lou Gehrig	1927	Yankees	.765
Babe Ruth	1923	Yankees	.764
Rogers Hornsby	1925	Cardinals	.756
Jimmie Foxx	1932	Athletics	.749

*CURRENT TO 1997

4.6 C. Joe Sewell of the Indians

Known as "the man who never struck out," Sewell developed his batting stroke as a boy in Alabama by throwing rocks and lumps of coal in the air and hitting them with a broomstick. He was blessed with such sharp eyes, he claimed that he could make out the seams on the ball as it neared the plate. Sewell fanned only 114 times in 7,132 career at-bats, a ratio of one strikeout per 63 at-bats. In 1929, he went a record 115 games (437 at-bats) in a row without striking out. In all, Sewell had five seasons in which he fanned four times or less in 500-plus at-bats.

4.7 B. Mel Ott

On October 5, 1929, the Phillies hosted the Giants in a double-header. Although neither team was in the pennant hunt, the twin bill still had an element of drama because the home run title was at stake. The Giants' Mel Ott and the Phillies' Chuck Klein began the day tied for the league lead with 42 homers each. In game one, Klein connected off Carl Hubbell, to break Roger Hornsby's NL record and move one ahead of Ott. In game two, to preserve Klein's lead, Philly pitchers walked Ott intentionally five times, the last free pass coming with the bases loaded! In his final game of the season against the Braves, Ott failed to hit a homer and finished second to Klein in the dinger derby.

4.8   D. Cincinnati's Crosley Field

On the night of May 24, 1935, President Franklin D. Roosevelt pushed a button in the White House that ignited 632 lamps at Cincinnati's Crosley Field. In the first major-league game played under artificial illumination, the Reds defeated the Phillies 2–1. The lights were installed at the urging of Reds general manager Larry MacPhail, who was convinced that night ball was the wave of the future. His view was not shared by baseball's conservative hierarchy, and Cincinnati was allowed to host only seven night games in 1935. Said Washington Senators owner Clark Griffith: "There is no chance of night baseball ever becoming popular in the bigger cities because high-class baseball cannot be played under artificial lights."

4.9   C. 26 innings

On May 1, 1920, Joe Oeschger of the Braves and Leon Cadore of the Dodgers battled each other for 26 innings—the equivalent of almost three full games—only to settle for a 1–1 tie. The marathon ended after three hours and 50 minutes, when umpire Barry McCormick called the game due to darkness. Amazingly, neither pitcher seemed any worse for the ordeal. Cadore posted a 15–14 record for the NL-champion Dodgers that year, the best mark of his career; Oeschger had a 15–13 record for the seventh-place Braves and won 20 games the next year.

4.10   B. Bubbles Hargrave of the Reds

Hargrave and Cuckoo Christensen of the Cincinnati Reds waged a season-long tussle for the NL batting crown in 1926, with Hargrave eventually winning .353 to .350. No catcher had won a batting title before then. Under today's rules, Hargrave would not have qualified for the honor because he only had 326 at-bats. But at the time a player was only required to appear in two-thirds of his team's games to be eligible, and Hargrave appeared in 68 percent (105 of the Reds' 154 games). Oddly, Christensen, Earl Smith and

Joe DiMaggio: He personified power, excellence and grace.

Cy Williams—the second-, third- and fourth-place finishers in the 1926 NL batting race—would all have failed to qualify by today's standards as well.

4.11   D. Tommy Holmes of the 1945 Braves

Holmes had a career year in 1945, batting .352 and topping the NL in hits (224), doubles (47), homers (28), total bases (367) and slugging average (.577). In addition to his torrid hitting, the Braves' outfielder also fanned just nine times in 636 at-bats, to become the only major leaguer to lead his league in homers and fewest strikeouts.

4.12   C. He led the NL in homers and stolen bases

Only two players have led their league in homers and stolen bases in the same year: Ty Cobb of the Tigers in 1909 (nine homers, 76 steals) and Chuck Klein of the Phillies. With just 79 career stolen bases to his credit, Klein would seem an unlikely candidate for the feat. Although he paced the NL in homers four times, he topped the circuit only once in thefts—in 1932, when he stole 20 bases. That year, Klein tied Mel Ott for the NL lead in homers with 38.

4.13   C. Joe DiMaggio

Joltin' Joe became the first rookie to play in an All-Star game, when he was named the AL's starting right fielder in 1936. DiMaggio played the entire game, going hitless in five at-bats. He would play every inning of seven straight All-Star games before his string ended in 1943, when he entered the armed forces. The only other individual to approach DiMaggio's mark is Detroit Tigers second baseman Charlie Gehringer, who played every inning of the first six All-Star games from 1933 through to 1938.

4.14   B. 1939

On August 26, 1939, station WX2XB made history with the first telecast of a major-league game between the Dodgers and the Reds at Ebbets Field. Red Barber called the action and conducted the first ever on-field interviews—with opposing managers Leo Durocher and Bill McKechnie. One camera was placed at ground level behind home plate and another in the upper deck above third base. The radius of the coverage was 40 miles. The event attracted little attention because there were only about 400 TV sets in all of New York. It was one of the few times in history that more people saw a sporting event in person than watched it on TV. Intrigued with the technology, Dodgers general manager Larry MacPhail continued to telecast one game a week from Ebbets Field during 1940 and 1941, until the onset of the war curtailed the experiment.

4.15   D. Win a batting title while playing for two teams

Despite leading the AL in hits as a rookie in 1929 and batting over .300 in each of his first three seasons, Dale Alexander was traded by the Detroit Tigers to the Boston Red Sox in June 1932. He proceeded to hit an AL-high .367, becoming the first player to win a batting title while playing for two teams. Alexander's promising career in Beantown came to a bizarre end in 1933, when the big first-sacker twisted an ankle during a game against the Athletics and had to leave the game for treatment. Team physician Doc Woods put Alexander's leg in a diathermy machine, but he became distracted by a Red Sox rally and forgot about his patient. By the time Woods returned to the clubhouse, Alexander had suffered third-degree burns. The burns developed into gangrene, and Alexander almost lost his leg. He was forced to retire at age 30, with a career average of .331.

4.16   D. Lou Gehrig

On July 4, 1939, 62,000 fans attended Lou Gehrig Day at Yankee Stadium. Brushing back tears, Gehrig, who was suffering from an incurable disease known as amyotrophic lateral sclerosis, gave his famous farewell speech that began with the words: "Fans, for the past two weeks you have been reading about a bad break I got. Yet today I consider myself the luckiest man on the face of the earth." During the ceremonies, Gehrig's No. 4 was retired—no previous player had received such an honour (Ruth's No. 3 was not retired by the Yankees until 1948)—and the rule was waived so that he could be inducted into the Hall of Fame without the usual waiting period. The Yankee hero died two years later, a few weeks short of his 38th birthday.

THE SULTAN OF SWAT

"To try to capture Babe Ruth with statistics would be like trying to keep up with him on a night out," wrote Bob Broeg of *The Sporting News*. We won't try to capture Ruth here, just pursue a few of his daytime exploits. Match the correct number with the corresponding achievement from the Sultan of Swat's storied career.

(Answers are on page 139)

Category	Number		
A. Batting crowns	0	1	2
B. MVP Awards	1	2	3
C. Rank on the all-time RBI list	1	2	3
D. 200-hit seasons	3	5	7
E. AL home-run titles	8	10	12
F. Seasons of 40-plus homers	9	11	13
G. World Series homers	12	15	18
H. Career stolen-base total	43	83	123
I. Career pitching wins	64	94	124
J. Most runs scored in a season	157	167	177

Mickey Cochrane:
The driving
force behind five
pennant winners.

Chapter Five

WHO AM I?

The 1934 All-Star game lived up to its billing—an amazing 17 of the game's 18 starters were later elected to the Hall of Fame. The one player who didn't make it was the National League's starting center fielder. Four years earlier, he had set the NL mark for most homers and most runs batted in by a rookie. After compiling 169 homers and 633 RBI in his first six seasons, he too appeared headed for Cooperstown, but his production tailed off after he hurt his shoulder in 1936. Who is he?

In this chapter, we alter the multiple-choice format and supply all 16 answers. Match the players listed below with their Who am I? descriptions. The remaining 17th name is our mystery All-Star.

(Answers are on page 66)

Pete Reiser	Eppa Rixey	Al Simmons	Floyd Giebell
Sam Rice	Hub Pruett	Cy Williams	Harlond Clift
Jim Tobin	Jeff Heath	Hack Wilson	Mickey Cochrane
Flint Rhem	Wally Berger	Wes Ferrell	Van Lingle Mungo
Lefty O'Doul			

5.1 When I hung up my spikes, I ranked seventh on the all-time hit list, but because I quit the game 13 hits shy of the 3,000 mark, I remain one of the more obscure Hall of Famers. **Who am I?**

5.2 I could really fire the old apple. I notched 238 strikeouts with Brooklyn in 1936, the most by an NL pitcher during the decade. Yet as hard as I threw, I drank even harder, which caused me loads of trouble. All told, I racked up $15,000 in fines, which is more than I ever earned in a season. **Who am I?**

5.3 I won 20 games six times and posted 193 career wins, but I was also handy with a bat. In 1931, I cracked nine homers, a single-season record for pitchers. I hit 38 four-baggers in my career, which is ten more than my brother the catcher did, and he's in the Hall of Fame and I'm not. **Who am I?**

5.4 At age 22, I hit .343 to become the youngest NL batting champ. I also led the loop in runs, doubles, triples and slugging average. Everyone expected me to enjoy a brilliant career, but my potential was never realized because I had a bad habit of running into outfield walls. **Who am I?**

5.5 Legend has it that I struck out Babe Ruth every time I faced him. Although that's an exaggeration, the truth is only slightly less impressive. In 1922, as a rookie with the St. Louis Browns, I fanned Ruth ten of the first 14 times I faced him. **Who am I?**

5.6 They called me "Bucketfoot" and said I'd never be able to hit major-league pitching. Twenty years and 2,927 hits later, they all had to eat their words. **Who am I?**

5.7 A serious beaning ended my playing days in 1937, but not before I had established my claim to being one of the greatest catchers of all time. No other backstop has ever matched my .320 career batting average. **Who am I?**

5.8 In 1938, I became the first third baseman in the majors to hit 30 homers in a season. In 1937, I handled 637 chances, an AL record

for my position. I also started 50 double plays, a record that
lasted until 1971. **Who am I?**

5.9 In 1942, I had one memorable game when I hit three home runs.
No other 20th-century pitcher has matched that feat. In 1944,
I did something nearly as unusual when I tossed a no-hitter and
hit a homer in the same game. **Who am I?**

5.10 From 1926 to 1930, I averaged 35 homers and 141 RBI a season.
But in 1931, booze got the better of me and my production dipped
dramatically. I played three more seasons, but my glory years
were behind me. **Who am I?**

5.11 In 1929, I drilled an NL-record 254 hits and batted .398. One more
hit would have given me a .400 average. Even so, many people
don't remember me. I may be better known in the Orient, where
I'm often called "the father of Japanese baseball." **Who am I?**

5.12 In 1933, I retired with 266 wins, the most by a lefty in National
League history at the time. Not many hitters took me deep.
In 1921, I allowed only one homer in 301 innings. **Who am I?**

5.13 Joe DiMaggio and Ted Williams stole the spotlight in 1941, but I
also did some damage with my lumber. I became the first AL player
to hit 20-plus doubles, triples and homers in a season. **Who am I?**

5.14 Rogers Hornsby was the only National Leaguer to hit more
homers than I did during the 1920s. I won four home-run titles,
the last in 1927, at age 39. **Who am I?**

5.15 I won just three games in the majors, but one was headline news.
On September 27, 1940, I beat Cleveland's Bob Feller 2–0 to
clinch the flag for the Detroit Tigers. **Who am I?**

5.16 I led the NL in wins with the Cardinals in 1926, but I'm best
remembered for a game I didn't pitch. On the eve of a key
contest versus the Dodgers in 1930, I was "kidnapped" by a
gang of gun-toting thugs. **Who am I?**

Answers

W H O   A M   I ?

5.1   Slap-hitting **Sam Rice** possessed little power (he hit only 34 homers in his career, and 21 were inside-the-park jobs), but he was a speedy runner and a superb outfielder. Rice reached the 200-hit mark seven times, including 207 hits at age 40, in 1930. In all, he compiled 2,987 hits in his 20-year career. Asked why he retired just 13 hits shy of 3,000, Rice explained: "You must remember, there wasn't much emphasis then on 3,000 hits. And to tell the truth, I didn't know how many hits I had when I quit."

5.2   Until he hurt his arm in 1937, **Van Lingle Mungo** was one of majors' hardest throwers. From 1934 to 1936, Dizzy Dean was the only NL pitcher who fanned more batters than the Dodger fireballer. But Mungo's off-field exploits often took center stage. A compulsive womanizer and boozehound (Leo Durocher claimed Mungo would drink anything, even hair tonic), Mungo's most notorious escapade occurred in 1941. The Dodgers were training in Cuba and staying at Havana's Nacional Hotel. One night, Mungo talked two women—the hotel singer, Lady Vine, and the female half of the Latin dance team Carrero and Carrero—into going to bed with him. Señor Carrero didn't appreciate the gesture, and when he found his wife in Mungo's room, a fight ensued. Mungo landed several punches, threw Carrero into the hallway and bolted the door. The enraged Cuban later returned with a machete, but by that time the Dodgers had spirited their pitcher out of the room and hidden him in the cellar. Police were soon swarming over the hotel with a warrant for Mungo's arrest. The Dodgers had to arrange for a seaplane to smuggle him out of Cuba.

Then they fined him and sent him to the minors. Mungo was also sued $20,000 for lost income by Señor Carrero, whose injuries prevented him from dancing for some time.

5.3 One of the best hitting pitchers of all time, **Wes Ferrell** clubbed 38 career homers, a record for moundsmen, and had a lifetime .280 batting average. In 1931, he stroked nine homers in only 116 at-bats. Ferrell also won 20 games six times, including four straight with the Indians from 1929 to 1932. He retired with 193 wins and a .601 winning percentage, and probably deserves to be in the Hall of Fame. His brother Rick, a catcher, made the Hall in 1984, despite hitting only 28 homers.

5.4 "Pistol" **Pete Reiser** had as much raw talent as anyone. Unfortunately, the Dodger outfielder played baseball like a kamikaze pilot. During his ten-year career, he was carried off the field 11 times. Reiser's nemeses were outfield walls—he crashed into them nine times. Seven times he broke his collarbone or dislocated a shoulder; twice he suffered skull fractures. The second was so severe that a priest administered the last rites over his body in the clubhouse. Reiser developed a sense of humor about his injuries. Before a 1946 exhibition game, a radio announcer was asking Dodger players where they thought they would finish that year. "First place," said Pee Wee Reese. So did Hugh Casey and Dixie Walker. When the announcer asked Reiser where he thought he'd finish the season, he replied, "In Peck Memorial Hospital."

5.5 Rookie **Hub Pruett** played a key role in the St. Louis Browns' run at the AL pennant in 1922. Used as a reliever and spot starter, the 21-year-old southpaw posted a 2.33 ERA, the best by any AL pitcher with more than 100 innings. But Pruett's main claim to fame was his uncanny success against Babe Ruth. Befuddling the great slugger with his screwball, Pruett fanned Ruth ten of the first 14 times he faced him, including twice with the bases loaded. In the other four at-bats, Ruth walked three times and had a weak ground out. It wasn't until their 15th encounter that Ruth got his first hit off Pruett, a home run. He followed that up with a single. All told, Pruett held the Bambino to an anemic .158 batting average in 1922.

Pruett developed a lame arm at the end of 1922 and was never as effective a pitcher again. Even so, Pruett lasted seven years in the majors, in no small part because of the reputation he earned against Ruth. He used his baseball savings to attend college and became a doctor. Years later when he met Ruth, he said, "I want to thank you for putting me through medical school. If it wasn't for you, no one would have heard of me."

5.6   Maybe the only player to be nicknamed because of his batting stance, right-handed swinging **Al Simmons** broke with convention by striding toward third base with his left leg as the pitcher delivered the ball—a move known as "stepping into the bucket." However unorthodox, the stance worked for "Bucketfoot Al," who cracked the 100-RBI mark a dozen times and posted a lifetime batting average of .334. No one called the hot-tempered Simmons "Bucketfoot" to his face. He detested the moniker because he felt it questioned his courage. As Simmons told one interviewer, "It made me sound like I was afraid of the ball. After awhile they stopped calling my by that name, because they knew it made me angry, and the angrier I got, the better I hit."

5.7   Detroit's player-manager **Mickey Cochrane** was struck in the head by a fastball thrown by pitcher Bump Hadley at Yankee Stadium on May 25, 1937. The impact shattered his skull in three places, and he hovered near death for four days. Black Mike recovered to resume his managing duties later that season, but his playing days were done. The injury brought down the curtain on a stellar career. The fiery Cochrane sparked the Philadelphia Athletics to three straight pennants from 1929 to 1931 and led the Tigers to back-to-back flags in 1934 and 1935 as a player-manager. He retired with a .320 lifetime batting average, the highest of any catcher.

5.8   The unlucky fate of **Harlond Clift** was to play for the St. Louis Browns during the 1930s, when the Browns were consistent losers and had the worst fan support of any team in history. This doomed Clift to obscurity even as he was putting up power numbers unmatched by any previous third baseman. He led all third-sackers in homers for four straight seasons from 1936 to 1939, and in

Al Simmons: He batted .363 through his first eight seasons.

1938, he hit 34 homers to become the first hot-corner man to top 30. Clift was also a fine fielder. In 1937, he participated in 50 double plays and had 405 assists, setting two records that lasted until Graig Nettles broke them in 1971. Even so, Clift was not named to an All-Star team during his 12-year career.

5.9   In 1942, Boston Braves pitcher **Jim Tobin** nearly hit six home runs in six consecutive at-bats in a three-day span versus the Chicago Cubs. He pinch-hit one over the fence, came back the next day to pinch-hit another one out of the yard, then went in the third day to pitch and in his first at-bat hit a long drive to the base of the center-field fence. In his next three plate appearances, Tobin clubbed three homers, the last a two-run shot in the eighth inning to win the game 6–5. In 1944, Tobin hit a homer and pitched a no-hitter in the same game, a feat managed by just two other pitchers: Catfish Hunter and Rick Wise.

5.10   From the waist up, **Hack Wilson** was built like a blacksmith, with a barrel chest and massive arms. But all that muscle was mounted on a stumpy pair of legs and tiny feet. He stood only five foot six, but weighed 190 pounds and had an 18-inch collar and size six shoes. A fan favorite, Wilson was the NL's top slugger in the late 1920s. In 1930, with the Cubs, he had a monster season, batting .356 with an NL-record 56 homers and an all-time record 190 RBI. But in 1931, hard-nosed Rogers Hornsby took over as manager. The two men clashed, and Wilson sulked and began drinking heavily. When his batting average plummeted to .261 and his homer output fell to 13, the Cubs dealt him to Brooklyn. Wilson made a modest comeback in 1932, hitting 23 homers and 123 RBI, but after that point his life went rapidly downhill. Out of baseball by 1935, he was reduced to handing out towels at a Baltimore pool when he died of a pulmonary edema and a sclerotic liver in 1948.

5.11   **Lefty O'Doul** began his career as a pitcher with the Yankees in 1919, but he flopped in that role. After being demoted to the minors in 1923, he switched to the outfield and enjoyed several stellar years with the San Francisco Seals of the Pacific Coast League. In 1928, he resurfaced in the majors. In 1929, with the

Phillies, he had his finest season, batting .398 with 152 runs, 122 RBI and an NL-record 254 hits. O'Doul retired in 1934 with a lifetime .349 batting average. He coached the PCL Seals until 1951, serving as a mentor for several major leaguers. Starting in 1930, O'Doul began making regular trips to Japan, where he helped organize that country's professional league and earned the title "the father of Japanese baseball."

5.12   At six foot five, **Eppa Rixey** towered over most of his contemporaries, but the big southpaw was not a power pitcher. Instead, he baffled hitters with his pinpoint control, changeups and breaking balls. In 1921, he allowed only one homer in 301 innings. From 1912 to 1933, Rixey racked up 266 wins with the Phillies and the Reds, the most by an NL lefty until Warren Spahn won his 267th in 1962.

5.13   **Jeff Heath** posted impressive numbers with the Cleveland Indians in 1941. The Canadian-born outfielder batted .340, led the AL in triples with 20 and amassed 343 total bases, only five less than league-leader Joe DiMaggio. Especially noteworthy were Heath's totals in doubles (32), triples (20) and homers (24). Only five players have ever reached the 20-plateau in all three categories, and Heath was the first AL player to do it.

20-PLUS DOUBLES, TRIPLES AND HOMERS IN A SEASON*

Player	Year	Team	2B	3B	HR
Frank Schulte	1911	Cubs	30	21	21
Jim Bottomley	1928	Cardinals	42	20	31
Jeff Heath	**1941**	**Indians**	**32**	**20**	**24**
Willie Mays	1954	Giants	26	20	35
George Brett	1979	Royals	42	20	23

*CURRENT TO 1997

5.14   A dead-pull, lefty hitter, **Cy Williams** had a swing ideally suited to Baker Bowl, his home park with the Phillies from 1918 to 1930. His best power year was 1923, when he hit 41 round-trippers. Williams won his fourth and last homer title in 1927, when he was two months shy of his 40th birthday. He was the first National Leaguer to swat 200 homers, a milestone he reached in 1926. Williams also owns the unusual distinction of playing for a different manager in each of his first 14 seasons in the bigs.

5.15   The Detroit Tigers were improbable AL champions in 1940, having finished 26½ games behind the Yankees in 1939, so it was fitting that a complete unknown should toss their pennant-clinching victory. Detroit visited Cleveland for the last three games of the season, clinging to a two-game lead over the Indians. The Tribe sent Bob Feller to the mound for the series opener; Detroit countered with **Floyd Giebell**, a 30-year-old rookie, who had recently been called up from the minors. The skinny West Virginian's big-league experience consisted of 24 innings. Tigers manager Del Baker later explained his logic to reporters. "I figured it would be to my best advantage to start Giebell against Feller, because if Feller is right, nobody beats him. So why waste a good pitcher trying?" Giebell confounded the odds by twirling a complete-game shutout, beating the Indians 2–0 and securing the flag for the Tigers. It was only his third major-league win, and, as it turned out, it was also his last. Giebell pitched poorly in 17 games in 1941 and was sent back to the minors, never to return.

5.16   In the heat of the 1930 pennant race, St. Louis visited Brooklyn for a key three-game series with the Dodgers. Cardinals manager Gabby Street picked pitcher **Flint Rhem** to start the series' opener, but at game time, Rhem was nowhere to be found. He showed up two days later in a condition described as "unbecoming a major-league player." Rhem claimed he'd been kidnapped by hoodlums who took him to their hangout in New Jersey and forced him to drink large amounts of liquor at gunpoint to prevent him from pitching against the Dodgers. "I kept begging them to let me go, but it was one drink after another," he moaned. The idea of anyone forcing a compulsive tippler like Rhem to drink alcohol was ludicrous, but Street opted not to fine his pitcher. Rhem recovered from his "ordeal" and won two games down the stretch to help the Cards capture the pennant.

G A M E 5

K E Y S T O N E   C O M B O S

Most successful teams have a shortstop and second baseman who are adept at turning double plays. Often, though, one member of the keystone combo is more famous than the other. Listed below are ten not-so-well-known infielders from pennant-winning clubs. Match them up with their more illustrious partners. *(Answers are on page 139)*

Mark Koenig   Joe Boley   Charlie Gelbert
Buddy Myer   Billy Jurges   Travis Jackson
Joe Gordon   Woody English   Billy Rogell
Tommy Thevenow

Team	Second Baseman	Shortstop
1. 1924 Giants	Frankie Frisch	_____
2. 1926 Cardinals	Rogers Hornsby	_____
3. 1927 Yankees	Tony Lazzeri	_____
4. 1929 Cubs	Rogers Hornsby	_____
5. 1930 Athletics	Max Bishop	_____
6. 1931 Cardinals	Frankie Frisch	_____
7. 1933 Senators	_____	Joe Cronin
8. 1935 Tigers	Charlie Gehringer	_____
9. 1935 Cubs	Billy Herman	_____
10. 1941 Yankees	_____	Phil Rizzuto

Lou Gehrig and
Babe Ruth:
They formed the
deadly heart of
Murderers' Row.

Chapter Six

MURDERERS' ROW
AND THE G-MEN

The name "Murderers' Row" is associated with the 1927 New York Yankees and the heavy-hitting heart of their batting order, but this was not the first Yankee club to wear the colorful tag. It was earlier applied to the 1920 squad, not just because Babe Ruth belted 54 homers, but because for the first time in history at least eight homers were credited to five members of one team: Ruth, Bob Meusel (11), Wally Pipp (11), Aaron Ward (11) and Roger Peckinpaugh (8). The 115 homers the Yankees hit in 1920 set a new American League record, but it was just a hint of the mayhem to come. In 1927, the Ruth–Gehrig-led Yankee juggernaut thumped 158 out of the park. *(Answers are on page 79)*

6.1 **Which pennant-winning club was led by a trio of talented performers known as "the G-Men"?**

A. The 1933 Washington Senators
B. The 1934 Detroit Tigers
C. The 1938 Chicago Cubs
D. The 1942 St. Louis Cardinals

6.2 **Why did Babe Ruth wear No. 3 with the Yankees?**
A. Because he was born on February 3
B. Because that was his lucky number
C. Because that was his spot in the batting order
D. Because the player he replaced wore No. 3

6.3 **In 1930, the New York Giants set the all-time record for the highest team batting average. What did the Giants hit?**
A. .299
B. .309
C. .319
D. .329

6.4 **From which team in the Pacific Coast League did the Yankees obtain Joe DiMaggio?**
A. The Oakland Oaks
B. The San Francisco Seals
C. The Hollywood Stars
D. The Sacramento Solons

6.5 **Which club wore an elephant emblem on its jerseys in the 1920s?**
A. The Brooklyn Dodgers
B. The New York Giants
C. The Philadelphia Athletics
D. The Washington Senators

6.6 **The term "five o'clock lightning" was associated with what team?**
A. The 1927 New York Yankees
B. The 1930 Chicago Cubs
C. The 1931 Philadelphia Athletics
D. The 1941 Brooklyn Dodgers

6.7 **Rogers Hornsby holds the single-season batting average record for how many different teams?**
A. Two
B. Three
C. Four
D. Five

6.8 During the 1930s, the St. Louis Cardinals were known as the Gashouse Gang. Virtually everyone on this zany team had a nickname. Who was "the Wild Hoss of the Osage"?

A. Joe Medwick
B. Rip Collins
C. Leo Durocher
D. Pepper Martin

6.9 How many consecutive seasons did Mel Ott lead the New York Giants in home runs?

A. Six
B. Ten
C. 14
D. 18

6.10 Which team failed to win the pennant despite having four 20-game winners on its pitching staff?

A. The 1920 Chicago White Sox
B. The 1924 New York Yankees
C. The 1926 Cincinnati Reds
D. The 1934 New York Giants

6.11 During the 1930s, the New York Yankees set a record for playing the most consecutive games without being shut out. In how many straight games did the Yankees score at least one run?

A. 108
B. 208
C. 308
D. 408

6.12 How old was Lou Boudreau when he was appointed player-manager of the Cleveland Indians in 1942?

A. 24
B. 27
C. 30
D. 33

6.13 **Who is the only player to hit as many homers as the rest of his team in three seasons?**

A. Wally Berger of the Braves

B. Jack Fournier of the Dodgers

C. Babe Ruth of the Yankees

D. Goose Goslin of the Senators

6.14 **Who was the last National League owner to manage his team for an entire season?**

A. Sam Breadon of the Cardinals

B. Barney Dreyfuss of the Pirates

C. Emil Fuchs of the Braves

D. Powell Crosley of the Reds

6.15 **Pitcher Bobo Newsom owns the dubious distinction of being traded more often than any other major leaguer. How often did Newsom switch teams during his 20-year career?**

A. 10 times

B. 13 times

C. 16 times

D. 19 times

6.16 **Which club changed its name to the Blue Jays in 1944?**

A. The Boston Braves

B. The St. Louis Browns

C. The Pittsburgh Pirates

D. The Philadelphia Phillies

6.17 **The Boston Red Sox are supposedly plagued by "the Curse of the Bambino." Which team is hexed by "the Billy Goat curse"?**

A. The Chicago Cubs

B. The Brooklyn Dodgers

C. The Philadelphia Phillies

D. The Washington Senators

ANSWERS

MURDERERS' ROW AND THE G-MEN

6.1 **B. The 1934 Detroit Tigers**
The 1934 Tigers had four players who racked up 100 or more RBI, and three of them—Hank Greenberg, Charley Gehringer and Goose Goslin—had last names that began with the letter G. The crack combo tormented AL pitchers all summer and helped spark Detroit to its first flag in 25 years. Inspired by the FBI agents who were making headlines in their battle against organized crime, sportswriters dubbed the trio "the G-Men."

6.2 **C. Because that was his spot in the batting order**
Although the Cleveland Indians and St. Louis Cardinals had both earlier experimented with numbers attached to players' sleeves, it was not until 1929 that the New York Yankees put numbers on their players' jersey backs on a permanent basis. Since team personnel and batting orders were relatively stable in those days, especially on the Yankees, their players (with the exception of the pitchers) were assigned numbers according to their spot in the batting order. As a result, Babe Ruth became No. 3 and Lou Gehrig No. 4.

6.3 **C. .319**
When baseball's moguls discovered how much the fans enjoyed power hitting, they began tinkering with the ball to increase its liveliness. In 1930, the juicing process reached its ultimate. Not only was the core of the ball given added resiliency, but the seams were also sewn flush to the cowhide, so pitchers could not get the same tight breaking action. Predictably, hitting exploded. Three of

the four best team batting averages of all time were posted in the NL in 1930. The New York Giants led the onslaught with a .319 average, the highest in history, while the Philadelphia Phillies hit .315 and the St. Louis Cardinals .314. Despite his club's success, Giants manager John McGraw had misgivings about the direction baseball was taking. He proposed deadening the ball and moving the pitcher's mound a few feet closer to the plate. "Youngsters in the amateur ranks and on the sandlots no longer have ambitions to become pitchers," said McGraw. "They want to play some other position in which they can get by without being discouraged."

THE HIGHEST TEAM BATTING AVERAGES OF ALL TIME*

Team	League	Year	Ave
New York Giants	NL	1930	.319
Detroit Tigers	AL	1921	.316
Philadelphia Phillies	NL	1930	.315
St. Louis Cardinals	NL	1930	.314
St. Louis Browns	AL	1922	.313
Chicago Cubs	NL	1930	.309
Pittsburgh Pirates	NL	1928	.309
Philadelphia Phillies	NL	1929	.309
New York Yankees	AL	1930	.309

*CURRENT TO 1997

6.4 B. The San Francisco Seals

Joe DiMaggio debuted at age 17, with the PCL Seals in 1933. He soon attracted the attention of big-league scouts by embarking on a torrid 61-game hitting streak. He finished the year with a .340 batting average, 28 homers and 169 RBI in 187 games. An encore performance was expected in 1934, but DiMaggio's season ended early when he tore the cartilage in one knee. The injury caused other teams to lose interest in him, but the Yankees persevered, eventually buying DiMaggio from Seals owner Charlie Graham on November 21, 1934, for $25,000 and five players. The Yankees protected themselves and sweetened the deal for Graham by allowing DiMaggio to play for the Seals in 1935, with the proviso that if his knee failed to hold up, then Graham could keep the players, but not the cash. DiMaggio's knee held up fine. He played in 172 games, collected 270 hits, drove in 154 runs and batted .398.

6.5 **C. The Philadelphia Athletics**

The link between elephants and the Athletics dates back to the turn of the century. In 1901, John McGraw managed the Baltimore Orioles of the newly formed American League, where he developed a dislike for the Philadelphia Athletics, a team managed by Connie Mack. When McGraw left the Orioles in 1902 to manage the National League's New York Giants, he derisively snapped, "It looks like the American League's got a white elephant in Philadelphia." To taunt McGraw, Mack adopted the term as his club's nickname, and when the Giants and Athletics met in the 1905 World Series, the A's jokingly presented McGraw with a toy white elephant. The moniker stuck, and in 1920, Mack removed the "A" from his team's jerseys and replaced it with a blue elephant. In 1924, Mack changed the color to white to comply with McGraw's original insult. Mack later restored the "A" to his team's shirt fronts, but the pachyderm image endured, and a rearing white elephant is still the Athletics' logo today.

6.6 **A. The 1927 New York Yankees**

During the 1920s, baseball games usually began at 3:30 P.M. Early in the 1927 season, the Yankees won several games with eighth- and ninth-inning rallies, which occurred about 5 P.M. Yankee center fielder Earle Combs picked up on this trend, and every day in the bottom of the eighth, whether the club was ahead or behind, he would come trotting in from the outfield yelling, "C'mon gang! Five o'clock lightning! Five o'clock lightning!" The Yankees often supplied the late-inning fireworks, and other teams soon came to dread the ominous phrase.

6.7 **B. Three**

From a pitcher's perspective, Rogers Hornsby was a fearsome sight. "You might not have liked what was on his mind," noted one hurler, "but you always knew damned well what it was." The greatest right-handed hitter of all time, Hornsby holds the single-season batting mark for three teams. He hit .424 for the Cardinals in 1924, .387 for the Braves in 1928 and .380 for the Cubs in 1929. At one point, Hornsby also held the single-season mark for a fourth NL club. His .361 average for the Giants in 1927 set a franchise high that lasted until 1930, when Bill Terry hit .401. That Hornsby could set four different teams' batting records in a span of six years is a testimony to his skill, but the fact each team opted to trade him also indicates how abrasive a personality he had.

6.8   D. Pepper Martin

Precisely when the term Gashouse Gang was first used in print is disputed, but in 1932, Warren Brown of the *Chicago Herald and Examiner* described Pepper Martin, whose uniform was perpetually dirty due to his reckless, headfirst slides, as looking "like a refugee from a gasworks." Martin, who played the game, according to one teammate, as if "he had electricity running up his ass," earned the nickname "the Wild Hoss of the Osage" when he played football for the Osage Indians in his native Oklahoma. A hard-running halfback, Martin was noted for his galloping gait. The chief wildman and joker of the raucous Gashouse Gang, he was fond of pranks such as tossing sneezing powder into hotel ventilation systems or sitting in his room and dropping water balloons on the heads of passers-by. Martin kept the Gashouse Gang loose, but his crazy antics also prompted manager Frankie Frisch to exclaim, "We could finish first or in an asylum."

6.9   D. 18

For 18 straight seasons, from 1928 to 1945, Mel Ott led the Giants in homers. Although he was only five foot nine and 170 pounds, Ott had a lot of pop in his bat, and his lefty swing was tailor-made for the Polo Grounds' short right-field porch. Master Melvin smacked 324 of his 511 career homers at home. The disparity became even more pronounced as Ott aged. In 1943, he hit 18 dingers at the Polo Grounds and none anywhere else. All told, Ott led the NL in homers six times and was runner-up seven times.

Mel Ott: He was the first NL player to hit 500 homers.

6.10   **A. The 1920 Chicago White Sox**
Only two major-league clubs—the 1971 Baltimore Orioles and the 1920 Chicago White Sox—have ever had four 20-game winners. The 1920 White Sox staff featured Red Faber (23–13), Lefty Williams (22–14), Eddie Cicotte (21–10) and Dickie Kerr (21–9). Yet, despite getting 87 wins from their big four, the Pale Hose failed to win the pennant, finishing two games behind Cleveland. For baseball's sake, it's fortunate Chicago didn't, because eight White Sox players were suspended late in the season after being accused of fixing the 1919 World Series. One can imagine the resulting turmoil if news of the scandal had broken with the White Sox representing the American League in the 1920 Series.

6.11   **C. 308**
After being blanked 1–0 by the Red Sox's Wilcy Moore on August 2, 1931, the Yankees went a record 308 consecutive games without being shut out. During that span, they scored 1,986 runs (6.4 per game) to 1,434 runs for the opposition. The streak ended nearly two years later to the day, when Lefty Grove of the Athletics tamed the Bronx Bombers 7–0, on August 3, 1933.

6.12   **A. 24**
Shortstop Lou Boudreau took over as the Indians player-manager in 1942, at age 24. It could not have been an easy assignment, as Boudreau was the youngest regular on the team. Boudreau inherited the managerial reins from Roger Peckinpaugh, who, ironically, is the only man to manage a major-league club at a younger age than Boudreau. In 1914, Peckinpaugh, a 23-year-old shortstop, served as player-manager of the Yankees for the last 17 games of the season after skipper Frank Chance was fired. The Indians finished with a 75–79 record under Boudreau in 1942, which was identical to the record they had with Peckinpaugh in 1941.

6.13   **A. Wally Berger of the Braves**
Since 1900, 16 players have had a season in which they hit as many homers as the rest of their team, but only two players have done it more than once: Babe Ruth with the Boston Red Sox in 1918 and

1919, and Wally Berger, who managed the feat three times with the Boston Braves. In 1930, Berger walloped 38 of his team's 66 homers; in 1931 he hit 19 of his team's 34 round-trippers; and in 1933, he accounted for 27 of his club's 54 circuit blasts. Spacious Braves Field was a challenging park for long-ball hitters, which only underscores Berger's prowess, but he was also surrounded by a cast of 98-pound weaklings. In 1930, when Berger cracked 38 four-baggers, Boston's second-best power hitter was Buster Chatham with five homers.

SUPPLYING 50% OF A TEAM'S HOME RUNS (1920–1945)

Player	Year	Team	Player's Homers	Teammates' Homers
Goose Goslin	1924	Senators	12	10
Cy Williams	1927	Phillies	30	27
Wally Berger	**1930**	**Braves**	**38**	**28**
Wally Berger	**1931**	**Braves**	**19**	**15**
Wally Berger	**1933**	**Braves**	**27**	**27**
Jimmie Foxx	1938	Red Sox	50	48
Bill Nicholson	1943	Cubs	29	23
Stan Spence	1944	Senators	18	15

6.14 C. Emil Fuchs of the Braves

Fuchs, a former judge and the deputy attorney of New York state, bought the Boston Braves in 1923, only to watch them finish last twice and second-last three times in the next six years. Tired of the Braves' losing ways, Fuchs appointed himself manager in 1929, saying, "The time has gone when a manager has to chew tobacco and talk from the side of his mouth. I don't think our club can do any worse with me as a manager than it has done the last few years." Unfortunately, Fuchs knew little about baseball. He declined to use the squeeze play, for example, insisting it wasn't an "honorable way" to score a run. He also had a habit of relating long-winded stories to his players in the midst of crucial game situations, much to the irritation of umpires. Whether the Braves played any better under Fuchs's command is debatable. The club lost five fewer games in 1929 than it had in 1928, but slipped from seventh place into the cellar. In 1930, Fuchs stepped down and Bill McKechnie took over as manager.

6.15 C. 16 times

Norman Louis Newsom sometimes answered to the name "Buck," but usually he was called "Bobo" because that was what he called everyone else. It's said that Newsom called everyone Bobo because he was rarely around long enough to learn their real names. A true baseball vagabond, Newsom pitched 20 years in the majors, but never spent more than three seasons with any team. In all, he changed uniforms 16 times. He played for nine clubs: the Dodgers, Cubs, Giants, Tigers, Browns, Yankees, Red Sox, Athletics and Senators. Newsom served five terms in Washington, which allowed him to boast that he beat Franklin Roosevelt's record by one.

6.16 D. The Philadelphia Phillies

After Phillies owner William D. Cox was banned from baseball for betting on his team's games in November 1943, the franchise was sold to Robert Carpenter, Sr., chairman of DuPont, for $400,000. Carpenter appointed his son Robert, Jr. to run the club. One of his first moves was to hold a fan contest to give the team a new name. The winning entry was the Blue Jays. Despite Carpenter's best efforts, the name never caught on, and in 1946 the team again officially became known as the Phillies.

6.17 A. The Chicago Cubs

During the 1945 World Series, a Chicago tavern owner named Billy Sianis arrived at the entrance to Wrigley Field with a box-seat ticket, but was denied admission into the park. Sianis was not allowed in because he had a goat with him. After being rebuffed, Sianis put a hex on the team, vowing they would never win another pennant. The Cubs have not won a flag since.

R A I S I N G   T H E   F L A G

Every pennant-winning club has some unique ingredient that propels
it to the top. Match each of these flag winners with its identifying
characteristic.   *(Answers are on page 139)*

1920 Indians	1930 Cardinals	1935 Cubs
1927 Yankees	1931 Athletics	1936 Yankees
1927 Pirates	1932 Yankees	1940 Reds

1. _____ Boasted the league's top three home-run
hitters.

2. _____ Compiled a 21-game winning streak in
September.

3. _____ Player-manager hit 50 doubles and
batted .388.

4. _____ Had a record five players top the 100-RBI
plateau.

5. _____ Led by two brothers who rapped
460 hits.

6. _____ All eight regulars in the lineup hit .300
or better.

7. _____ Top four pitchers posted an 87–27
won–lost record.

8. _____ Registered a winning percentage of
.805 at home.

9. _____ Won 43 of their 100 victories by one run.

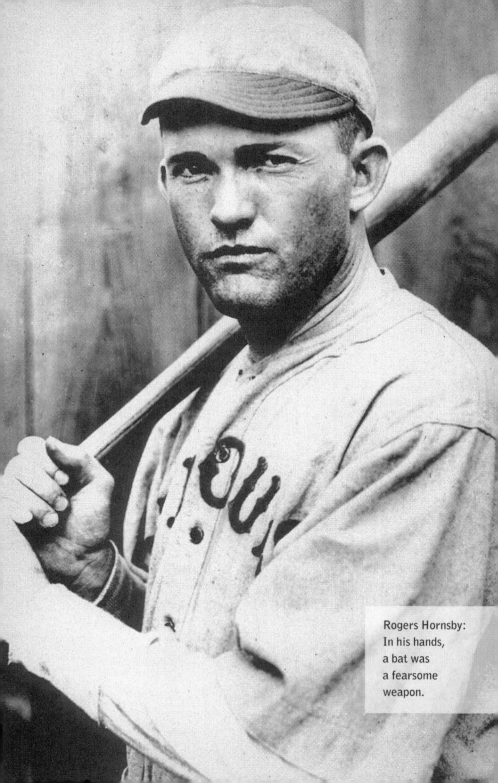

Rogers Hornsby:
In his hands,
a bat was
a fearsome
weapon.

Chapter Seven

BOUND FOR COOPERSTOWN

Asked once what he did in the offseason, Rogers Hornsby replied: "I'll tell you what I do. I stare out the window and wait for spring." Aside from gambling, baseball was his sole passion. He did not smoke or drink, or even read or watch movies for fear it would hurt his batting eye. Nor did the cold-eyed Texan have any close friends, preferring to room alone. What gave Hornsby joy was hitting the daylights out of a baseball, which he did with astonishing regularity. From 1921 to 1925, through 696 games and 2,679 at-bats, he averaged a .402 batting mark. That hallucinatory figure wasn't inflated by cheap singles—he led the NL in slugging average in each of those five years. Fittingly, when Hornsby was elected to the Hall of Fame in 1942, he was the year's only inductee. *(Answers are on page 93)*

7.1 **The Baseball Hall of Fame inducted its first five players in 1936. Who was the leading vote getter?**

A. Honus Wagner

B. Ty Cobb

C. Babe Ruth

D. Christy Mathewson

7.2 Babe Ruth belted 714 home runs in his career. What percentage of that total did he hit after turning 30 years old?
A. 30 percent
B. 40 percent
C. 50 percent
D. 60 percent

7.3 After 30 seasons as manager of the New York Giants, John McGraw resigned midway through the 1932 campaign. Which future Hall of Famer replaced him as the Giants' skipper?
A. Mel Ott
B. Bill Terry
C. Casey Stengel
D. Fred Lindstrom

7.4 Who is the only player to smash three homers in back-to-back World Series?
A. Goose Goslin
B. Babe Ruth
C. Jimmie Foxx
D. Hank Greenberg

7.5 Nolan Ryan and Steve Carlton rank one-two in career strikeouts, with 5,714 and 4,136. At age 22, Ryan had 231 strikeouts and Carlton had 214. How many Ks did Bob Feller have at age 22?
A. 333
B. 633
C. 933
D. 1,233

7.6 Of all the players with 300 career home runs, who has the best homer-to-strikeout ratio?
A. Ted Williams
B. Johnny Mize
C. Joe DiMaggio
D. Rogers Hornsby

7.7 How many ERA titles did Lefty Grove win in his career?
A. Five
B. Seven
C. Nine
D. 11

7.8 Who is the only catcher to win two batting titles?
A. Bill Dickey
B. Mickey Cochrane
C. Ernie Lombardi
D. Gabby Hartnett

7.9 Who is the only Hall of Famer to crack a homer in his first
major-league at-bat on opening day?
A. Earl Averill
B. Al Simmons
C. Tony Lazzeri
D. Bobby Doerr

7.10 Which hard-drinking Hall of Famer did Casey Stengel describe
as "a very graceful player, because he could slide without
breaking the bottle in his hip pocket"?
A. Paul Waner
B. Earle Combs
C. Tris Speaker
D. Goose Goslin

7.11 How many games did Dizzy Dean win in his career?
A. 150
B. 200
C. 250
D. 300

7.12 Which second baseman was dubbed "the Mechanical Man"?
A. Eddie Collins
B. Frankie Frisch
C. Billy Herman
D. Charlie Gehringer

7.13 **Who is the only player to twice amass 420 total bases in a season?**
A. Babe Ruth
B. Lou Gehrig
C. Chuck Klein
D. Jimmie Foxx

7.14 **Which of the following career pitching records belongs to Walter Johnson?**
A. Most shutouts
B. Most complete games
C. Most ERA titles
D. Most 20-win seasons

7.15 **Which Hall of Fame pitcher won 260 games in his career, yet never logged 100 strikeouts in a season?**
A. Ted Lyons
B. Waite Hoyt
C. Red Ruffing
D. Burleigh Grimes

7.16 **Who was known as "the black Babe Ruth"?**
A. Buck Leonard
B. Pop Lloyd
C. Josh Gibson
D. Mule Suttles

7.17 **Which Hall of Famer holds the American League record for most RBI in a season?**
A. Babe Ruth
B. Lou Gehrig
C. Ted Williams
D. Hank Greenberg

Answers

BOUND FOR COOPERSTOWN

7.1   **B. Ty Cobb**
Although construction of the National Baseball Hall of Fame was not completed until 1939, the Baseball Writers Association of America elected the Hall's first five inductees on February 2, 1936. Ty Cobb received the most votes, as he was named on 222 of 226 ballots. Babe Ruth and Honus Wagner tied for second with 215, while Christy Mathewson received 205 and Walter Johnson 189. Although Ruth's star later eclipsed Cobb's as baseball's greatest player, in the eyes of their contemporaries, it was the irascible Cobb who deserved the honour.

7.2   **D. 60 percent**
The popular image of Babe Ruth as a pot-bellied guy with spindly legs belies Ruth's natural athleticism. In spite of his infamous drinking, eating and carousing, Ruth displayed remarkable longevity. Most players' power numbers begin to tumble when they reach age 30, but the Bambino still had several big years ahead of him, including 60 home runs in 1927, at age 32. He hit an incredible 430 homers from age 30 onward, as opposed to 284 before. Ruth hit more circuit clouts after turning 30 than Joe DiMaggio, Duke Snider or Al Kaline did in their entire careers.

7.3   **B. Bill Terry**
On June 1, 1932, Giants manager John McGraw beckoned first baseman Bill Terry into his office and told him to shut the door. The two men had been locked in a sullen feud and hadn't spoken in more than a year, so Terry assumed McGraw was going to

inform him he had been traded. Instead, McGraw surprised him by saying: "I'm retiring from this job. If you want it, you can have it." Terry accepted the offer on the spot. The 59-year-old legend pinned a message on the bulletin board announcing his resignation and walked out. In his tenure as the Giants' skipper, McGraw won three World Series and ten pennants. He returned only once to the Giants' clubhouse—to congratulate Terry on winning the 1933 pennant. McGraw died of prostate cancer in 1934.

7.4 A. Goose Goslin

Nicknamed Goose because of his long nose and his last name, Leon Goslin secured a spot in World Series lore by smashing three homers for the Washington Senators in the 1924 and 1925 Fall Classics. Other players have hit three home runs in more than one Series, but no one else has done it in back-to-back years. Although Goslin hit only 248 homers in his 18-year career, this was due more to do with where he played than a lack of power. Washington's Griffith Stadium, Goslin's home field for the first nine years of his career, was the worst home-run park in baseball for a left-handed hitter. From 1921 to 1929, Goslin hit only 24 homers at home, compared with 84 on the road. In any other AL park he would have been poling 30 to 40 homers a year. After he was traded to the St. Louis Browns in 1930, Goslin hit 37 four-baggers.

7.5 D. 1,233

When facing Bob Feller, Senators manager Bucky Harris would tell his batters: "Go up there and hit what you see. If don't see anything, come on back." Considering his awesome velocity, it is surprising to discover that Feller's 2,581 strikeouts does not rank among the top 15 totals of all time. However, the sum is deceiving. When Feller joined the navy a month after his 23rd birthday in December 1941, he had already fanned 1,233 batters. At the same age, Sandy Koufax had 313 strikeouts, Nolan Ryan, 231, and Steve Carlton, 214. It's intriguing to speculate how many Feller might have recorded if he had not missed four prime years, from ages 23 to 26. He logged 260 strikeouts in his last peace-time year and 348 in his first full season after returning from the war. It's reasonable to assume that had he played in those lost years, he would have fanned another 1,200 batters (an average of 300 a season), which would give him 3,781 Ks, the third-best of all time. He might have also set the single-season mark for strikeouts. It's impossible to say. However, it's entirely possible that AL hitters never saw the best of "Rapid Robert" Feller.

7.6 **C. Joe DiMaggio**

Modern-day sluggers typically whiff two or three times as often as they hit one out of the park. In comparison, Joe DiMaggio's career homer-to-strikeout ratio seems otherwordly. The Yankee Clipper hit 361 homers while fanning only 369 times, close to an average of one homer for every strikeout. The only other member of the 300-homer club remotely close to DiMaggio's ratio is Yogi Berra, with 358 homers and 415 strikeouts. In 1941, the year of his 56-game hitting streak, DiMaggio fanned just 13 times in 541 at-bats, while drilling 30 homers and 125 RBI.

BEST CAREER HOMER-TO-STRIKEOUT RATIO (300 HR OR MORE)

Player	AB	HR	SO	Ratio
Joe DiMaggio	6,821	361	369	.978
Yogi Berra	7,555	358	415	.863
Ted Williams	7,706	521	709	.735
Johnny Mize	6,443	359	524	.685
Stan Musial	10,972	475	696	.682
Lou Gehrig	8,001	493	789	.625
Chuck Klein	6,486	300	521	.576
Mel Ott	9,456	511	896	.570

7.7 **C. Nine**

Although Lefty Grove didn't make the majors until age 25 and pitched during a hitting-dominated era, he still posted some mesmerizing numbers. Grove paced the AL in strikeouts for seven consecutive years, from 1925 to 1931, and rang up seven straight 20-win seasons, from 1927 to 1933. He also led the AL in winning percentage a record five times. Yet perhaps the best indicator of his excellence is his nine ERA crowns. No other pitcher has ever won more than five. In five of his chart-topping seasons, Grove was the only AL pitcher to post an ERA under 3.00. His 2.06 ERA in 1931 was 2.32 runs below the league average, an AL record.

LEFTY GROVE'S ERA CROWNS

Year	Team	W	L	ERA	AL ERA
1926	Athletics	13	13	2.51	4.02
1929	Athletics	20	6	2.81	4.24
1930	Athletics	28	5	2.54	4.65
1931	Athletics	31	4	2.06	4.38
1932	Athletics	25	10	2.84	4.48
1935	Red Sox	20	12	2.70	4.45
1936	Red Sox	17	12	2.81	5.04
1938	Red Sox	14	4	3.08	4.79
1939	Red Sox	15	4	2.54	4.62

7.8 C. Ernie Lombardi

A ferocious line-drive hitter who dented walls in every National League city, Lombardi would have posted a higher career batting average than .306 if he had possessed even ordinary speed. But the huge catcher moved like a tank. Opposing infielders would play him so deep that they were standing on the outfield grass. Lombardi once told Dodger shortstop Pee Wee Reese, "You'd been in the league five years before I learned you weren't an outfielder." Lombardi's best season was 1938, when he batted .342 for the Cincinnati Reds to take the batting crown. Even though the Reds finished fourth, the lumbering catcher was voted MVP. In 1942, Lombardi hit .330 with the Boston Braves to become the only backstop to win two batting titles.

7.9 A. Earl Averill

The Cleveland Indians rookie kicked off his career with a bang, belting a homer in his first at-bat on opening day of the 1929 season. Averill, who would drill 237 more four-baggers before he was done, earned entry to Cooperstown in 1975. The only other Hall of Famer to hit a home run in his first at-bat was pitcher Hoyt Wilhelm in 1952, but Wilhelm did not connect on opening day.

7.10   A. Paul Waner

Waner often played drunk or hung over and slyly admitted there was a certain advantage to it: a pitched ball looked so blurry to him at times there was "more of it to hit." An intelligent man with a wry sense of humor, Waner once observed, "They say money talks. All it's ever said to me is 'good-bye.'" Waner's affinity for alcohol had remarkably little effect on his batting stroke. He registered eight 200-hit seasons and won three NL batting titles in his 20-year career, retiring with 3,152 career hits and a .333 batting average.

7.11   A. 150

Excluding black inductees, no other Hall of Famer won as few games as Dizzy Dean. His career spanned 12 seasons, but in three of those years—the first and the last two—he pitched only one game. Essentially, Dean's career consisted of nine seasons, and of those, his Hall of Fame credentials are based on the five years from 1932 to 1936, when he logged 130 of his 150 wins. A fractured toe that Dean suffered when he was struck in the foot by a line drive at the 1937 All-Star game effectively ended his career. Instead of waiting for the broken digit to heal, Dean was soon back on the mound. But to compensate for the pain and discomfort he felt, he altered his pitching motion and hurt his arm. Dean's famous fastball suddenly vanished, never to return, and at age 26, he was finished as a dominant pitcher.

7.12   D. Charlie Gehringer

Consistency was Gehringer's middle name. As Tiger teammate Doc Cramer said about him: "All you have to do is wind him up on opening day, and he runs on and on, doing everything right all season." A seamless defensive player and artful hitter, Gehringer posted stunning offensive numbers for a second baseman. Seven times he topped the 200-hit mark, hit 40-plus doubles and had more than 100 RBI. Twelve times he scored more than 100 runs. Voted AL MVP in 1937, Gehringer had a career batting average of .320.

7.13 C. Chuck Klein

Of the eight players who have amassed 420 total bases or more in a season, Chuck Klein is the only one to do it twice. While playing with the Phillies, Klein compiled 445 bases in 1930, and 420 in 1932. In his first five full seasons, Klein was the best all-purpose hitter in the senior circuit. At various times, he held the 20th-century NL single-season records for runs, doubles and homers, and assists by an outfielder. The assist and run records still belong to him. He hit .300 or more nine times (seven times consecutively), led the NL in homers four times and won a Triple Crown. Yet many of his achievements were devalued because he played in a hitter's park. Klein had to wait until 1980 before the Veterans Committee finally bowed to public pressure and voted him into the Hall of Fame.

MOST TOTAL BASES IN A SEASON*

Player	Year	Team	1B	2B	3B	HR	Total
Babe Ruth	1921	Yankees	135	29	8	60	457
Rogers Hornsby	1922	Cardinals	148	46	14	42	450
Lou Gehrig	1927	Yankees	101	52	18	47	447
Chuck Klein	**1930**	**Phillies**	**143**	**59**	**8**	**40**	**445**
Jimmie Foxx	1932	Athletics	113	33	9	58	438
Stan Musial	1948	Cardinals	127	46	18	39	429
Hack Wilson	1930	Cubs	111	35	6	56	423
Chuck Klein	**1932**	**Phillies**	**123**	**50**	**15**	**38**	**420**

*CURRENT TO 1997

7.14 A. Most shutouts

Walter Johnson tossed his last shutout in 1927. It gave the sidearm slinger a career total of 110, the most of any pitcher in history. Because Johnson spent his entire career with the punchless Washington Senators, he often needed to hold the opposition scoreless to win. An amazing 38 of Johnson's shutouts were 1–0 scores. He also lost 26 games by 1–0 scores. In 1913, "the Big Train" blanked opposing hitters for 55⅔ consecutive innings, the equivalent of more than six straight shutouts.

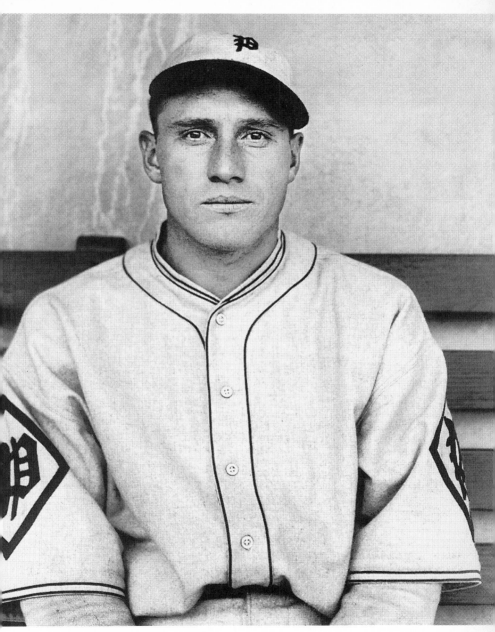

Chuck Klein: He won the NL Triple Crown with the Phillies in 1933.

7.15 A. Ted Lyons

Elected to the Hall of Fame in 1955, Lyons won 260 games in a 21-year career spent entirely with the Chicago White Sox. For much of that time, Chicago was entrenched in the AL's second division, yet Lyons still posted three 20-win seasons. Had he been with the Yankees, he might have won 400 games. A finesse pitcher, Lyons averaged about two strikeouts per nine innings during his career and never came close to fanning 100 batters in a season. His high was 74 Ks in 228 innings in 1933.

7.16 C. Josh Gibson

A barrel-chested catcher with huge arms and a quick, compact swing, Gibson was black baseball's greatest home-run hitter. He led the Negro Leagues in homers ten times. In 1931, he slammed more than 70 homers in Negro League play and exhibition games. Like Ruth, many of Gibson's blasts were tape-measure shots. He is reputed to have hit the longest homers in several big-league parks, including Yankee Stadium. *The Sporting News* credits Gibson with a drive at Yankee Stadium that hit just two feet from the top of the wall above the center-field bleachers, 580 feet from the plate. Some swear Gibson once hit a fair ball over the left-field roof in Yankee Stadium. In 1943, with the Homestead Grays, he belted 11 homers at Washington's spacious Griffith Stadium—more than the entire Washington Senators team hit there that season. Gibson died in 1947, the year Jackie Robinson broke the major-league color barrier. Had the color line been lowered a decade earlier, he would undoubtedly have become one of the majors' greatest stars. Gibson was elected to the Hall of Fame in 1972.

7.17 B. Lou Gehrig

A lethal hitter with men on base, Gehrig produced an AL-record 184 RBI in 1931. In 13 full seasons, the Yankee slugger averaged 147 RBI a year. Since the Iron Horse's retirement in 1939, only six players have exceeded that total in a single season.

GAME 7

F A B U L O U S   F E A T S

All of the Hall of Famers listed below have numerous entries in the record books, but we're only looking for one achievement per player here. Match the hitter and his claim to fame:

(Answers are on page 139)

Babe Ruth	Jimmie Foxx	Lou Gehrig	Ted Williams
Ty Cobb	Joe Medwick	Hank Greenberg	Rogers Hornsby
Tris Speaker	George Sisler	Joe DiMaggio	Al Simmons

1. _____ Rapped a single-season record 257 hits.

2. _____ Captured back-to-back MVP Awards.

3. _____ Banged out a career record 793 doubles.

4. _____ Won an unmatched six RBI titles.

5. _____ Bagged the most total bases by a Triple Crown winner.

6. _____ Logged a single-season record .551 on-base average.

7. _____ Led his league in hits eight times.

8. _____ Belted a career record 23 grand slams.

9. _____ Had more homers than strikeouts seven times.

10. _____ Drilled 40 or more doubles seven years in a row.

11. _____ Recorded 11 multiple-home-run games in a season.

12. _____ Posted the most hits in a season by a right-handed batter.

101

Bob Feller:
Few hitters
could catch up
to his explosive
fastball.

Chapter Eight

TRUE OR FALSE?

Bob Feller was still in high school when he tied the major-league record for most strikeouts in a game. True or False? It's true. Feller was only 17 years old when he tied Dizzy Dean's mark by fanning 17 batters in a 5–2 win over the Philadelphia Athletics on September 13, 1936. In doing so, he became the only pitcher to equal his age with strikeouts in a game. "I guess that's when people began to realize I was for real," said Feller. Unreal is more like it. With his 100-mile-per-hour fastball and hellacious curve, the teenager was a supernatural force. Feller, who joined the Cleveland Indians in August, ended his rookie campaign with a 5–3 won–lost record, 3.34 ERA and 76 strikeouts in 62 innings. He then returned home to Van Meter, Iowa, studied hard and graduated from high school.

(Answers are on page 106)

8.1   Babe Ruth was the first player to hit a home run at Yankee Stadium. **True or False?**

8.2   Ty Cobb's number was *not* retired by the Detroit Tigers. **True or False?**

8.3 No major leaguer has ever batted .400 and hit 40 homers in a season. **True or False?**

8.4 Jimmie Foxx hit more homers by age 30 than any other player in history. **True or False?**

8.5 Babe Ruth never pitched for the New York Yankees. **True or False?**

8.6 Ted Williams is the only player to win a Triple Crown and *not* be voted his league's MVP. **True or False?**

8.7 The New York Yankees adopted pinstriped uniforms because the team's owners thought they would make Babe Ruth look slimmer. **True or False?**

8.8 The New York Giants won pennants in 1922, 1923 and 1924, without having a single 20-game winner. **True or False?**

8.9 The team that holds the single-season record for most hits finished in last place. **True or False?**

8.10 Lou Gehrig once held the major-league record for the most consecutive games played at one position. **True or False?**

8.11 Until 1931, batted balls that bounced over an outfield fence in fair territory were counted as home runs. **True or False?**

8.12 Joe DiMaggio stole more bases in his career than Babe Ruth. **True or False?**

8.13 The oldest player to hit a homer in the majors was a pitcher. **True or False?**

8.14 Yankee Stadium was *not* the park where Babe Ruth hit his highest total of home runs in a season. **True or False?**

8.15 Jimmie Foxx's .364 batting average in 1932 is the highest by a player who hit 50 or more homers. **True or False?**

8.16 The Baby Ruth candy bar was named after Babe Ruth. **True or False?**

8.17 The record for most hits allowed in a game is held by a relief pitcher. **True or False?**

8.18 Babe Ruth never managed or coached in the majors. **True or False?**

8.19 Night baseball began in the minor leagues. **True or False?**

8.20 Ted Williams never collected 200 hits in a season. **True or False?**

8.21 Lou Gehrig holds the major-league record for most home runs by a first baseman. **True or False?**

8.22 Joe McCarthy was the first manager to win a World Series in both leagues. **True or False?**

8.23 Babe Ruth, Joe DiMaggio and Ted Williams once played together on the same team. **True or False?**

8.24 Babe Ruth hit three homers in his last game. **True or False?**

Answers

8.1 True

A crowd of 74,217 jammed into Yankee Stadium to witness the first game at the ballpark on April 18, 1923. Before the contest, Babe Ruth told a reporter, "I'd give a year of my life if I can hit a home run in this first game in this new park." In the third inning, with two runners aboard, Ruth realized his wish, smashing a shot into the right-field bleachers. Making it even sweeter, the blow came against Ruth's former team, the Boston Red Sox, and it proved the winning margin in a 4–1 Yankee victory.

8.2 True

Ty Cobb's number was not retired by the Tigers because he never wore one. Numbered uniforms did not become mandatory in the American League until 1931, three years after Cobb retired.

8.3 False

In 1922, Rogers Hornsby slammed 42 homers and batted .401 with the St. Louis Cardinals. No other major leaguer has ever hit 40 homers and batted .400. Hornsby came close to duplicating the feat in 1925, when he batted .403 with 39 homers. This stunning fusion of power and high average is especially remarkable, considering that Hornsby was a second baseman.

8.4 True

If Jimmie Foxx had maintained his power stroke for a few more years, he would rank higher than ninth on the home run list. By age 30, the muscular slugger had drilled 429 four-baggers, more than any other player has registered at that age. But Foxx went into a rapid decline after the 1940 season, when he hit 36 homers at age 32, giving him exactly 500 for his career. Foxx hit only 34 more before retiring in 1945. His decline was likely due to his fondness for liquor. He was as hard a drinker as he was a hitter.

MOST HOME RUNS BY AGE 30*

Player	HR	Season	Career Total
Jimmie Foxx	429	1938	534
Mickey Mantle	404	1962	536
Eddie Mathews	399	1962	512
Frank Robinson	373	1966	586
Mel Ott	369	1939	511
Hank Aaron	366	1964	755
Harmon Killebrew	336	1966	573
Ralph Kiner	329	1953	369
Willie Mays	319	1961	660
Duke Snider	316	1957	407

*CURRENT TO 1997

8.5 False

Babe Ruth had five pitching stints with the Yankees, four as a starter and one in relief, earning wins in all five games. His last mound appearance occurred in the final game of the 1933 season. Although he was 39 and had pitched only once in the previous 12 seasons, Ruth went the distance against the Red Sox, winning 6–5.

8.6 False

Ted Williams was not elected MVP in either of his two Triple Crown years, losing on both occasions to Yankees: Joe Gordon in 1942 and Joe DiMaggio in 1947. However, Williams is not the only Triple Crown winner to be snubbed in MVP voting. In 1933, the Phillies' Chuck Klein claimed the NL Triple Crown with a .368 average, 28 homers and 120 RBI, but lost to Giants pitcher Carl Hubbell, who was 23–12 with a 1.66 ERA. In 1934, Lou Gehrig led the AL in the three categories with a .363 average, 49 homers and 165 RBI, yet MVP honors went to catcher Mickey Cochrane of the Tigers, who hit .320 with just two homers and 76 RBI. Incredibly, Gehrig placed fifth in the balloting.

8.7   False

The Yankees first donned pinstripes in 1912, eight years before Babe Ruth joined the team. Although the Yankees are identified in many people's minds with pinstripes, they were not the first club to introduce the style. Pinstripes of various widths were already in vogue by the time they first appeared on a Yankee player.

8.8   True

The New York Giants won three straight NL flags during the 1920s without a single hurler reaching the 20-win mark. In 1922, Art Nehf topped the Giants' staff with 19 victories; in 1923, Rosy Ryan and Jack Scott paced the club with 16 wins; in 1924, Jack Bentley and Virgil Barnes led the team with 16 wins.

8.9   True

The 1930 Philadelphia Phillies amassed a single-season record 1,783 hits, yet still finished last, 40 games out of first. Three Phils topped the 200-hit mark—Chuck Klein (250), Pinky Whitney (207), Lefty O'Doul (202)—and the team batting average was an eye-popping .315. However, the Phillies' pitching was abysmal. Les Sweetland posted an ERA of 7.71 in 167 innings of work, and Claude Willoughby wasn't far behind with a 7.59 ERA in 153 innings. Philadelphia's staff had a collective ERA of 6.71, the worst in the 20th century.

8.10   False

Unlike Cal Ripken, Lou Gehrig did not play all the games of his iron-man streak at the same position. Although primarily a first baseman, Gehrig also played nine games in the outfield. His longest string of consecutive games at first base was 885, set between June 6, 1925 and September 27, 1930. The streak ended when Gehrig played left field in Babe Ruth's spot, when Ruth pitched the last game of the 1930 season. The mark for the most consecutive games at one position during Gehrig's era belonged to Everett Scott, who played 1,307 straight games at shortstop from June 20, 1916 to May 5, 1925.

8.11 True

Before 1931, a ball didn't have to leave the field in the air to count as a home run. Although Babe Ruth did not bounce any of his 60 homers over the fence in 1927, this forgotten rule puts a new spin on the argument that Roger Maris's record of 61 homers in 1961 is tainted because he set it in a 162-game season, instead of a 154-game schedule as Ruth did. Maris bounced at least two balls over the fence in 1961. They counted as ground-rule doubles. If Maris had been batting alongside Ruth in 1927, those two hits would have given him the record in 151 games.

8.12 False

Joe DiMaggio never stole more than six bases in a season and swiped only 30 in his 13-year career. Babe Ruth's best base-stealing seasons were 1921 and 1923, when he swiped 17. The total of those two years alone is greater than DiMaggio's career sum. Ruth retired with 123 thefts.

8.13 True

Pitcher Jack Quinn of the Philadelphia Athletics owns the distinction of being the oldest player to hit a homer in the majors. Quinn stroked a four-bagger a week before his 47th birthday against the St. Louis Browns on June 27, 1930. Quinn holds several age-related records. He is the oldest pitcher to win a game (49), start a World Series game (47), finish a World Series game (48) and lead in a major pitching category—saves, in 1932 (49). Quinn is also the oldest player to collect more than one hit in a season. In 1932, at age 49, he rapped four hits with the Brooklyn Dodgers.

8.14 True

Had the Yankees stayed in the Polo Grounds and not moved to Yankee Stadium in 1923, Ruth's career home-run total would have been even higher. Although it was a whopping 475 feet to dead center, the Polo Grounds had short foul lines: 280 feet in left and only 258 feet in right—a chip shot for a left-handed pull-hitter like Ruth. In 1920, Ruth hit 29 homers at the Polo Grounds; in 1921, he hit 32 round-trippers there in 255 at-bats, a ratio of one homer for every eight at-bats. In contrast, his single-season high at Yankee Stadium was 29 homers, in 1928. As Ruth said: "I cried when they took me out of the Polo Grounds."

8.15 False

Jimmie Foxx had a monster year in 1932, cranking out 58 homers and batting .364, but this is not the best batting average posted by a player with 50 homers. In 1921, Babe Ruth hit 59 homers and batted .378; in 1920, he hit 54 homers and batted .376.

BEST BATTING AVERAGES/50 HOMERS OR MORE*

Player	Year	Team	HR	AVE
Babe Ruth	1921	Yankees	59	.378
Babe Ruth	1920	Yankees	54	.376
Jimmie Foxx	1932	Athletics	58	.364
Babe Ruth	1927	Yankees	60	.356
Hack Wilson	1930	Cubs	56	.356
Mickey Mantle	1956	Yankees	52	.353
Jimmie Foxx	1938	Red Sox	50	.349
Babe Ruth	1928	Yankees	54	.323

*CURRENT TO 1997

8.16 False

Contrary to popular belief, the Baby Ruth chocolate bar was not named after Babe Ruth, but rather in honor of President Grover Cleveland's daughter Ruth. At one point, the Bambino did agree to endorse a new product called Babe Ruth's Home Run Candy, but the Curtiss Candy Corporation, makers of the Baby Ruth chocolate bar, appealed to the patent office, claiming that the new product would impinge on their bar's name. The patent office agreed, and the plans for Ruth's candy endorsement were shelved.

8.17 True

As a cost-saving measure, Athletics manager Connie Mack took a skeleton crew of 15 players, including just two pitchers, to Cleveland for a game on July 10, 1932. When starter Lew Krausse was shelled in the first inning, Mack summoned 35-year-old Eddie Rommel in from the bullpen. The A's reliever was in for a long afternoon—the slugfest lasted 17 innings before the A's finally eked out a 18–17 win. Rommel was pummeled for 14 runs and a single-game record 29 hits. It was Rommel's last major-league win and his last major-league appearance, but one he would probably just as soon forget.

8.18 False

Babe Ruth never managed in the majors, but he did come out of retirement to take a coaching post with the Brooklyn Dodgers in 1938. The Bambino was paid $15,000 to take batting and fielding practice, play in exhibitions and coach first base. Ruth knew that Dodger skipper Burleigh Grimes was going to be replaced at the season's end, and he hoped to be named as his replacement. When the job went to Leo Durocher, Ruth retired, this time for good.

8.19 True

Long before the first night game was played in the majors in 1935, clubs in the minors and Negro Leagues had already pioneered the concept. The first team to install a permanent lighting system was the Des Moines Demons of the Western League, who began playing nocturnal games on a regular basis in 1930. That same year, J.L. Wilkinson, owner of the Negro Leagues' Kansas City Monarchs, constructed a portable lighting system that he took on the road with his team.

8.20 True

Despite his majestic .344 career batting average, Ted Williams never compiled 200 hits in a season—not even in 1941, when he batted .406. He undoubtedly would have reached the mark if he had not been so selective a hitter. He walked 20 percent of the times he stepped to the plate, the highest ratio of anyone in history.

8.21 True

Lou Gehrig belted 493 homers, a record for first basemen. Jimmie Foxx ranks second on the first-sacker power chart with 473. Although Foxx hit 534 homers in his career, 61 of them came while he was stationed either at third base, at catcher or in the outfield.

8.22 False

Joe McCarthy was the first skipper to capture a flag in both leagues. However, McCarthy never won a World Series in the senior loop. Sparky Anderson was the first to manage a World Series champion in both leagues, winning with the Cincinnati Reds in 1975 and 1976 and with the Detroit Tigers in 1984.

8.23 True

On July 12, 1943, an exhibition game was held in Boston to raise funds for the war effort. The Boston Braves met an armed forces All-Star squad managed by Babe Ruth that featured Joe DiMaggio batting third and Ted Williams in the cleanup spot. The 48-year-old Ruth pinch-hit in the eighth inning and flied out. Williams won the contest with a three-run homer. Prior to the game, Williams and Ruth squared off in a home-run hitting duel. The Splendid Splinter drilled three. Ruth failed to reach the seats.

8.24 False

Babe Ruth, who played his last season with the Boston Braves, hit three homers versus the Pittsburgh Pirates on May 25, 1935, a week *before* his retirement. His third homer of the day, the 714th of his career, was a tremendous clout that cleared the grandstand roof in right field. It was the first ball hit out of Forbes Field, and it traveled an estimated 600 feet. The epic blast would have been a fitting farewell and Ruth wanted to retire after the game, but he had promised Braves owner Emil Fuchs that he would play in Cincinnati and Philadelphia, the next two stops on the road trip. His final appearance came against the Phillies during the first game of a doubleheader on May 31, 1935. After grounding out in the first inning, he hurt his knee chasing a fly in the bottom of the frame and left the game. He never played again. Sadly, Ruth's career ended not with a bang in Pittsburgh, but with a whimper in Philadelphia.

GREAT PRETENDERS

In each of the quartets below, there is one name that does not belong.
See if you can spot the bogus player.   *(Answers are on page 139)*

1. Won a Triple Crown:
    Lou Gehrig, Joe Medwick, Chuck Klein, Babe Ruth

2. Hit 40 homers in a season:
    Hal Trosky, Joe Medwick, Ted Williams, Chuck Klein

3. Won an NL MVP Award:
    Mel Ott, Frankie Frisch, Marty Marion, Dolf Camilli

4. Won an AL MVP Award:
    Joe Gordon, Charlie Gehringer, Spud Chandler, Al Simmons

5. Collected 3,000 career hits:
    Rogers Hornsby, Tris Speaker, Paul Waner, Stan Musial

6. Won 30 games in a season:
    Jim Bagby, Lefty Grove, Dizzy Dean, Carl Hubbell

7. Pitched a no-hitter:
    Lefty Grove, Carl Hubbell, Ted Lyons, Wes Ferrell

8. Served as a player-manager:
    Pie Traynor, Leo Durocher, George Sisler, Earl Averill

9. Hit three homers in one World Series:
    Lou Gehrig, Charlie Keller, Joe DiMaggio, Goose Goslin

10. Is a member of the Hall of Fame:
    Bob Meusel, Chick Hafey, Kiki Cuyler, Babe Herman

Hack Wilson: "Built like a beer keg and not unfamiliar with its contents."

Chapter Nine

OUTSIDE THE LINES

Hack Wilson was one of baseball's most notorious drinkers, yet he prided himself on his restraint. "I never played drunk," he claimed. "Hung over, yes, but never drunk." Unfortunately, his monstrous hangovers were equally problematic. Team trainers often had to douse Wilson in ice water to get him into playing condition. Cubs manager Joe McCarthy once tried to demonstrate to Wilson how drinking was harmful to his health. McCarthy dropped a worm into a glass of water and another into a glass of whiskey. As the liquor-soaked worm expired, he asked Wilson if had learned anything from the demonstration. "Yes," replied Wilson. "If you drink whiskey, you won't get worms."

In this chapter, we explore some other baseball-related events that took place outside the white lines. *(Answers are on page 119)*

9.1 **A major scandal nearly erupted in 1926, when which two future Hall of Famers were accused of betting on baseball games?**
A. Babe Ruth and Herb Pennock
B. Ty Cobb and Tris Speaker
C. Al Simmons and Mickey Cochrane
D. Rogers Hornsby and Pie Traynor

9.2   **What was the main reason for outlawing the spitball in 1920?**
A. It was considered unsanitary
B. It was considered a danger to batters
C. It was considered too difficult to hit
D. It was considered too difficult to catch

9.3   **What did New York Giants manager John McGraw describe as "the stupidest idea in baseball"?**
A. Team mascots
B. Night baseball
C. Relief-pitching specialists
D. The minor-league farm system

9.4   **For what reason did baseball commissioner Kenesaw Mountain Landis suspend Babe Ruth for the first six weeks of the 1922 season?**
A. For demanding a raise
B. For assaulting an umpire in spring training
C. For playing exhibition games in the offseason
D. For making critical remarks about Landis

9.5   **What innovation did National League president John Heydler propose in 1928 to improve baseball?**
A. Interleague play
B. Player names on uniforms
C. A postseason playoff system
D. The use of a designated hitter for the pitcher

9.6   **Which major leaguer led a double life, working as a spy for the U.S. government before and during World War II?**
A. Harry Craft
B. Moe Berg
C. George McQuinn
D. Jimmy Bloodworth

OUTSIDE THE LINES: QUESTIONS

9.7 After winning the AL batting crown with an average of .420 in 1922, George Sisler was sidelined for the entire 1923 season with what ailment?

A. Malaria

B. Blood poisoning

C. A sinus infection

D. A gunshot wound

9.8 Which baseball executive pioneered the ideas of night games, season-ticket sales and radio and TV broadcasts of his team's home games?

A. Tom Yawkey

B. Larry MacPhail

C. Phil Wrigley

D. Branch Rickey

9.9 Bill Veeck, Jr. tried unsuccessfully to buy the Philadelphia Phillies in the winter of 1943. What did Veeck intend to do with the team if he became owner?

A. Move the club to Los Angeles

B. Hire Babe Ruth as manager

C. Stock the team with players from the Negro Leagues

D. Change the team's name to the Firebirds

9.10 How did pitcher Hugh Casey stir up trouble at the Brooklyn Dodgers training camp in Havana, Cuba, in 1942?

A. He set fire to his team's hotel

B. He was caught cheating at a casino

C. He was photographed with mobsters

D. He got into a fistfight with novelist Ernest Hemingway

9.11 Who earned eight battle stars during World War II?

A. Bob Feller

B. Rudy York

C. Ted Williams

D. Pee Wee Reese

9.12 **Which piece of equipment underwent a major modification at the start of the 1943 season?**
A. The baseball
B. The baseball bat
C. The baseball cap
D. The baseball glove

9.13 **When he retired in 1928, Ty Cobb was a millionaire, not from his baseball earnings, but because he had bought stock in what product?**
A. Spalding sporting goods
B. Singer sewing machines
C. Coca-Cola
D. Ford motor cars

9.14 **How did Cincinnati Reds catcher Willard Hershberger make headlines in 1940?**
A. He shot and killed his wife
B. He committed suicide in midseason
C. He was arrested for robbing a bank
D. He invented a new type of catcher's mitt

Answers

O U T S I D E   T H E   L I N E S

9.1 **B. Ty Cobb and Tris Speaker**

In 1926, former pitcher Dutch Leonard contacted AL president Ban Johnson with evidence that he, Ty Cobb, Tris Speaker and "Smoky" Joe Wood had conspired to fix a game between the Detroit Tigers and the Cleveland Indians on September 25, 1919. Leonard produced letters written to him by Cobb and Wood that outlined details of a wager on a baseball game. Johnson paid Leonard $20,000 for the letters and told Cobb and Speaker that he would keep the scandal quiet if they resigned as managers. Both did so. The two stars were also released as players. But the story did not disappear. AL owners forced Johnson to turn the letters over to commissioner Kenesaw Mountain Landis, who issued a press statement outlining Leonard's charges and held a hearing to uncover the truth. Cobb and Speaker denied the accusations; Leonard, fearful of Cobb's wrath, declined to attend the hearing. Two months later, Landis exonerated Cobb and Speaker, stating, "These players have not been, or are they now, found guilty of fixing a ballgame." Cobb later claimed that his attorneys had "dictated" Landis's ruling by threatening to "tear baseball apart" with evidence of other gambling scandals if they were not acquitted. Cobb and Speaker returned to play two more years and were later elected to the Hall of Fame, but neither was ever invited to remain in baseball as a manager or in any other official position.

9.2 **A. It was considered unsanitary**

The spitball was outlawed on February 9, 1920, along with other trick pitches that involved defacing or applying foreign substances to the ball. Although the spitball was difficult to hit, the main impetus for banning the pitch was its unsanitary image—it was regarded as a health hazard. Baseball's arbiters took action against the spitball in the midst of a public-health crisis similar to today's AIDS scare. The culprits in those days were influenza, tuberculosis and cholera. In 1919, sanitariums were filled with people suffering from these illnesses, which doctors knew could be spread by saliva. When baseball banned the spitter, it didn't do it cold turkey. Seventeen spitball pitchers were exempted from the ban and allowed to continue throwing the wet one to the end of their careers.

9.3 D. The minor-league farm system

When Branch Rickey became general manager of the St. Louis Cardinals in 1917, he faced a vexing problem—his floundering club had little cash to buy young players from minor-league teams, which operated as independent entities, and no place to send prospects for seasoning. Rather than buying talent, Rickey resolved to grow his own. He convinced owner Sam Breadon to use some of the money he'd earned from the 1920 sale of the Cardinals' ballpark, Robison Field, to buy minor-league franchises. Rickey gradually began to amass a network of minor-league teams created and run purely to produce talent for the Cardinals, as well as surplus players who could be sold at a profit. John McGraw called Rickey's plan "the stupidest idea in baseball." Of course, McGraw had the luxury of buying talent for his wealthy Giants. But he wasn't the only critic. Commissioner Kenesaw Mountain Landis denounced Rickey system as "un-American." Nonetheless, his farm system paid off handsomely. St. Louis became a league power, winning nine pennants in 20 years. By the late 1930s, the Cardinals were affiliated with 30 minor-league teams, owning half of them, and had 800 players under contract. Soon, all major-league teams were following Rickey's example.

9.4 C. For playing exhibition games in the offseason

Early in the century it was common for players from World Series teams to capitalize on their celebrity by embarking on exhibition tours after the season, during which they would replay the Series in backwater towns. Baseball owners frowned on the practice, because they felt it would cheapen the allure of the real World Series. In 1911, the owners passed a rule forbidding players from Series teams from appearing in postseason exhibition games. Ruth was aware of the rule, but since barnstorming was such a big part of his income, he decided to stage a tour after the 1921 Series with teammates Bob Meusel and Bill Piercy, despite a warning from commissioner Kenesaw Mountain Landis. Ruth later cut the tour short at the urging of Yankee management, but it didn't help his cause. Accusing them of "mutinous defiance," Landis fined Ruth, Meusel and Piercy their World Series shares ($3,362 each) and suspended them for the first six weeks of the 1922 season.

9.5 **D. The use of a designated hitter for the pitcher**

At the annual winter meeting in December 1928, NL president John Heydler proposed a dramatic rule change—the establishment of a "tenth man," a pinch-hitter who would bat in place of the pitcher for the entire game. Heydler argued that the innovation would speed up the game and eliminate weak-hitting pitchers. In a mirror reversal of what occurred in 1973, the NL voted in favor of the change but the AL said no. Because of the AL's opposition, Heydler's "tenth man" idea died on the drawing board.

9.6 **B. Moe Berg**

Catcher Moe Berg was a very unusual major leaguer. In an era when many players were illiterate, he had graduated *magna cum laude* from Princeton University and spoke ten languages (although it was said he couldn't hit in any of them). In 1929, while playing for the Chicago White Sox, he earned a law degree and joined a Wall Street firm. But even stranger was Berg's offseason activity—he was a spy. In 1934, he accompanied Babe Ruth, Lou Gehrig and other all-stars on an exhibition trip to Japan, where he delivered the welcoming speech in Japanese and also addressed the Japanese legislature. But not all Berg's activities were so diplomatic. One day he feigned illness, left the team and climbed to the top of a Tokyo bell tower to take secret reconnaisance photos. They were later used by the U.S. government to compile aerial maps for the massive B-25 firebombing of Tokyo in 1942. After 15 years in the majors, Berg retired in 1939. Soon afterward he joined the Office of Strategic Services (OSS), an intelligence agency created to spy on enemy nations and sabotage their war potential. During World War II, he was assigned the task of going behind enemy lines to discover how close Nazi scientists were to creating an atomic bomb. In 1946, Berg was awarded the Medal of Freedom, the highest military honor given to civilians.

9.7   C. A sinus infection

George Sisler of the St. Louis Browns was the best contact hitter in baseball from 1920 to 1922. In those three seasons, the slick-fielding first baseman averaged 240 hits and twice topped the .400 mark. But after batting a colossal .420 in 1922, Sisler was stricken with influenza in January 1923, which resulted in a severe sinus infection. The affliction damaged his optic nerves and for a time he saw double. After missing the 1923 season, Sisler rejoined the Browns in 1924. He hit .305, a respectable average for many players, but a drop of more than 100 percentage points from his 1922 performance. Although he posted three more 200-hit seasons, Sisler's vision was not as sharp after the infection and he never again approached the rarefied realm of .400. He retired in 1930, with a .340 career average.

9.8   B. Larry MacPhail

Before entering baseball, MacPhail was employed as a lawyer, a car dealer, a banker and a department store executive. A natural promoter with visionary ideas, he also happened to be loud, belligerent, erratic and an alcoholic. "With no drinks he was brilliant," noted one sportswriter. "With one he was a genius. With two he was insane. And rarely did he stop at one." During front-office stints in Cincinnati and Brooklyn, MacPhail was responsible for pioneering most of the major innovations in baseball during the 1930s and 1940s, including night baseball, season-ticket sales, radio broadcasts of his team's home games, televised games and air travel for teams.

9.9   C. Stock the team with players from the Negro Leagues

In 1943, Bill Veeck, Jr. made an offer to purchase the debt-ridden Philadelphia Phillies from owner Gerry Nugent. Veeck planned to

George Sisler: The Browns' first baseman batted a sizzling .420 in 1922.

rejuvenate the cellar-dwelling Phillies by stocking the team with stars from the Negro Leagues. However, Veeck felt obligated to inform commissioner Kenesaw Mountain Landis of his intentions. Landis quickly killed the scheme. A few days later, NL president Ford Frick awarded the franchise to lumber magnate William Cox for half of Veeck's offering price. Had Veeck been allowed to proceed, the results could have been truly revolutionary. With Satchel Paige, Josh Gibson, Roy Campanella, Monte Irvine and other black stars in the lineup, the Phillies might well have won the pennant in the war-weakened NL.

9.10   D. He got into a fistfight with novelist Ernest Hemingway
At the Dodgers' training camp in Havana in 1942, Hemingway hosted a few of the Brooklyn players at his hacienda. After several drinks, Hemingway hauled out boxing gloves and challenged his guests to spar a few rounds. Casey was the only one to take him up on the challenge. When Casey floored Hemingway, the enraged novelist booted the Dodger pitcher in the testicles. Hemingway later urged Casey to stay the night and fight a duel with pistols in the morning. Casey wisely declined. Oddly, the two men became friends after the incident. Even odder, both later committed suicide with guns—Casey in 1951 and Hemingway in 1961.

9.11   A. Bob Feller
Although Feller qualified for a deferment from the military because his father was dying of cancer and was too ill to run the family farm, he joined the navy immediately after Pearl Harbor. Disdaining the preferential treatment available to him as baseball star, Feller opted for combat duty and saw plenty of it as the chief of a gun crew aboard the USS *Alabama*, a 35,000-ton battleship. Feller fought in naval engagements at Tarawa, Guam, Saipan, Iwo Jima and other blood-and-thunder Pacific outposts, earning eight battle stars.

9.12   A. The baseball
Because the two traditional sources of rubber, the Far East and Southeast Asia, were in the hands of Japan, the United States' wartime enemy, baseball's moguls tried to develop an alternative to the cork- and rubber-centered baseball. In 1943, the A.G. Spalding

Company introduced the "balata ball," named after a tree in the West Indies that produces a milky latex used in electrical insulation. The balata ball was a huge dud—it had the resiliency of a rock. Eleven shutouts were recorded in the first 29 games of the season. On May 9, after only nine homers were hit in 72 AL games, the balata ball was taken out of circulation.

9.13 C. Coca-Cola

Unlike most players, Ty Cobb didn't depend entirely on baseball for his money. By the 1920s, he owned stock in oil, cotton and automobiles. But the investment that paid Cobb the biggest dividends was one he made in 1918, when he bought $10,000 worth of shares of a fizzy soda that had been invented by an Atlanta pharmacist. The drink was called Coca-Cola. By 1927, Cobb's annual income from Coke had reached $350,000. He would later triple that sum by buying additional stock. In time, Cobb came to own 22,000 shares of the world's most popular soft drink.

9.14 B. He committed suicide in midseason

On August 3, 1940, Cincinnati Reds backup catcher Willard Hershberger, who had been playing in place of injured Ernie Lombardi, failed to show up for the first game of a doubleheader versus the Boston Braves. Gabe Paul, the team's traveling secretary, called his room at Boston's Copley Plaza Hotel. "I'm sick and can't play," said Hershberger, "but I'll come out right away anyway." When the game ended and he still hadn't arrived, another call was placed to his room. This time there was no answer. Dan Cohen, a friend of Hershberger, was dispatched to the hotel. Cohen found Hershberger slumped dead over the bathtub—he had slashed his throat with a razor. Hershberger left no suicide note, but several Reds players had noticed that he had been depressed recently. In fact, three days earlier Hershberger had told manager Bill McKechnie that he felt he was letting the team down and couldn't take the pressure of being the club's starting catcher. Hershberger is the only active major leaguer to commit suicide in the 20th century, but he was not the only suicide in his family. Hershberger's father shot himself in the family bathroom three weeks after the stock market crash in 1929.

A   C U T   A B O V E

When is hitting .370 more impressive than batting .400? It all depends on what the league hits that year. For example, when Bill Terry hit .401 in 1930, the National League average—pitchers and bench warmers included—was a rousing .303. When Chuck Klein hit .368 for the Phillies in 1933, the NL average was a more modest .266. If you subtract the league average from each player's batting average, you find that Klein outhit the senior circuit by a larger margin than Terry—.102 to .098. In relative terms, Klein had the better year.

So, who posted the largest single-season batting differential between 1920 and 1945? Two players—Rogers Hornsby and Ted Williams—are a cut above. Hornsby's .424 average in 1924 was .141 higher than the NL's .283 average. Williams's .406 average in 1941 was .140 better than the AL average of .266.

LARGEST BATTING DIFFERENTIALS (1920–1945)

Player	Year	Team	Player Average	League Average	Margin
Rogers Hornsby	1924	Cardinals	.424	.283	.141
Ted Williams	1941	Red Sox	.406	.266	.140
George Sisler	1922	Browns	.420	.284	.136
George Sisler	1920	Browns	.407	.283	.124
Harry Heilmann	1923	Tigers	.403	.282	.121
Harry Heilmann	1927	Tigers	.398	.285	.113
Al Simmons	1931	Athletics	.390	.278	.112
Rogers Hornsby	1925	Cardinals	.403	.292	.111
Babe Ruth	1923	Yankees	.393	.282	.111

Hornsby's 1924 performance and Williams's 1941 effort rank among the top ten largest batting differentials of the 20th century. Ty Cobb dominates the list, with three of the top four placings.

LARGEST BATTING DIFFERENTIALS (1901–1997)

Player	Year	Team	Player Average	League Average	Margin
Ty Cobb	1911	Tigers	.420	.273	.147
Ty Cobb	1912	Tigers	.410	.265	.145
Nap Lajoie	1901	Athletics	.422	.277	.145
Ty Cobb	1910	Tigers	.385	.243	.142
Nap Lajoie	1910	Indians	.384	.243	.141
Rogers Hornsby	1924	Cardinals	.424	.283	.141
Ted Williams	1941	Red Sox	.406	.266	.140
Tris Speaker	1916	Indians	.386	.248	.138
George Sisler	1922	Browns	.420	.284	.136
Nap Lajoie	1904	Indians	.381	.245	.136

If you subscribe to the theory that the overall talent level in baseball has increased since the game's early days, then Williams's 1941 showing may the best of all. If you add power hitting to the equation, then Williams would get the nod. His slugging average was .735 in 1941. No other player on the chart cracked .700.

Of course, if you start talking about slugging average and league differentials, then there's only one name that matters — Babe Ruth. In 1920, Ruth's slugging average was .847 and the AL average was .387. That's a differential of .460.

No other player has ever outslugged his league by a margin of more than .370. Ruth's performance in 1920 is more than a cut above. It's a jumbo-sized slice.

Pepper Martin: Always a fierce competitor, he was a buzzsaw in postseason play.

Chapter Ten

THE SERIES

Some players perform best when the stakes are highest. Pepper Martin loved pressure. In three World Series with the St. Louis Cardinals, the Oklahoma fireball hit .418, an all-time high for the Fall Classic. Martin's star shone brightest in the 1931 Series, when the rookie outfielder personally dismantled the Philadelphia Athletics. Martin drilled 12 hits, scored five times, drove in five runs and stole five bases—all in the first five games. Although his bat cooled off in games six and seven, Martin had one more heroic moment in the finale, snuffing out an A's rally by making a running, one-handed grab of Max Bishop's smoking liner with two on and two out in the ninth to preserve the Cardinals' 4–2 victory.

In this last chapter, we shine the spotlight on some of the era's other notable World Series performers. *(Answers are on page 133)*

10.1 **Which of these firsts did not occur during the 1920 World Series between the Cleveland Indians and the Brooklyn Dodgers?**

A. The first Series grand-slam homer

B. The first Series triple play

C. The first Series homer by a pitcher

D. The first Series game called due to darkness

10.2 **Which Yankee hurler pitched three complete games without allowing an earned run during the 1921 Series?**
A. Carl Mays
B. Jack Quinn
C. Waite Hoyt
D. Bob Shawkey

10.3 **Game one of the 1923 clash between the Yankees and Giants was played in the newly built Yankee Stadium. Who won the game by hitting a dramatic homer with two outs in the ninth?**
A. The Yankees' Babe Ruth
B. The Yankees' Bob Meusel
C. The Giants' George Kelly
D. The Giants' Casey Stengel

10.4 **What object played a key role in the Washington Senators' victory in the final game of the 1924 Series versus the New York Giants?**
A. An equipment bag
B. A stray pebble
C. A cloth banner
D. A pair of binoculars

10.5 **Pittsburgh's triumph in the 1925 Series was aided by the record eight errors committed by which Washington infielder?**
A. Bucky Harris
B. Joe Judge
C. Buddy Myer
D. Roger Peckinpaugh

10.6 **The pivotal moment of the 1926 Series occurred in game seven, when Cardinals reliever Grover Alexander fanned Tony Lazzeri of the Yankees with two outs and the bases loaded. In which inning did this famous showdown take place?**
A. Sixth inning
B. Seventh inning
C. Eighth inning
D. Ninth inning

10.7 Many regard the 1927 Yankees as the most awesome offensive machine of all time. How many homers did Ruth and company hit against the Pirates in the 1927 championship tilt?

A. None

B. Two

C. Six

D. Ten

10.8 The Yankees pulverized the Cardinals in the 1928 Series, scoring 27 runs in a four-game sweep. Who led the barrage, compiling an all-time record 1.727 slugging average?

A. Babe Ruth

B. Lou Gehrig

C. Bob Meusel

D. Tony Lazzeri

10.9 Which Philadelphia Athletics pitcher fanned a record 13 Chicago Cubs in the first game of the 1929 Fall Classic?

A. Billy Shores

B. Lefty Grove

C. Rube Walberg

D. Howard Ehmke

10.10 Babe Ruth's "called-shot" homer during the 1932 Series is one of the most famous and controversial events in baseball history. Which Chicago Cubs pitcher surrendered this epic blast?

A. Charlie Root

B. Guy Bush

C. Pat Malone

D. Burleigh Grimes

10.11 Play had to be halted during game seven of the 1934 Series when Detroit fans began pelting a St. Louis Cardinal player with garbage. Who was the target of their abuse?

A. Joe Medwick

B. Rip Collins

C. Leo Durocher

D. Frankie Frisch

10.12 The Yankees set a single-game record for runs versus the Giants in the second game of their 1936 showdown. How many runs did the Bronx Bombers push across the plate?

A. 12

B. 15

C. 18

D. 21

10.13 Which Yankee rookie supplied the firepower in the 1939 Series, scoring eight runs, belting three homers, driving in six runs and batting .438, as New York swept the Cincinnati Reds?

A. Red Rolfe

B. Babe Dahlgren

C. Charlie Keller

D. Tommy Henrich

10.14 Cincinnati catcher Jimmie Wilson was the surprise star of the 1940 Series between the Reds and the Tigers. Why was Wilson such an unlikely hero?

A. He was 49 years old

B. He hit just .168 during the season

C. He played with a fractured wrist

D. He had been the Reds' third-base coach for three years

10.15 Which Brooklyn Dodgers catcher wore the goat horns in the 1941 Series after he fumbled a game-ending third strike in game four, opening the door to a ninth-inning Yankee rally?

A. Herman Franks

B. Mickey Owen

C. Babe Phelps

D. Billy Sullivan

Answers

THE SERIES

10.1 D. The first Series game called due to darkness

The 1920 Series featured several firsts, all of which occurred during the fifth game and all of which were performed by members of the Cleveland Indians. They included the first Series triple play, an unassisted effort by second-baseman Bill Wambsganns; the first Series grand slam, by outfielder Elmer Smith; and the first Series homer by a pitcher, starter Jim Bagby. However, none of the games in the Series was called due to darkness.

10.2 C. Waite Hoyt

Hoyt pitched in six World Series with the Yankees during the 1920s, but he was never sharper than in his first in 1921. The 22-year-old righty faced the Giants three times in the best-of-nine affair, pitching three complete nine-inning games without allowing an earned run. His effort matched Christy Mathewson's Series record of 27 consecutive innings without an earned run, set in 1905. Hoyt beat the Giants 3–0 on a two-hitter in game two and 3–1 in game five, but lost a 1–0 squeaker in the decisive eighth game, when the Giants' Dave Bancroft scored on a first-inning error.

10.3 D. The Giants' Casey Stengel

Although the Yankees won the 1923 Series, they lost the first post-season game played at Yankee Stadium on a dramatic two-out, ninth-inning, inside-the-park homer by Giants outfielder Casey Stengel. Stengel also hit the second Series homer at Yankee Stadium, a drive into the right-field bleachers, to win game three for the Giants 1–0. Those were the Giants' only two wins in the

Series, so Stengel was stunned when he was traded to the Boston Braves in the off-season. As he told reporters: "I don't understand it. I just hit .417 in the Series with two game-winning homers. I guess I should count myself lucky that I didn't hit a third homer. They might have sent me to Topeka."

10.4   B. A stray pebble

The thrilling 1924 Series was ultimately decided by rough ground. In game seven, with two outs and the bases loaded, the Giants led the Senators 3–1 in the bottom of the eighth inning when Washington's Bucky Harris hit a sharp grounder toward third-baseman Fred Lindstrom. The ball hit a pebble and bounded over Lindstrom's head, sending home two runs to knot the game. The two teams were still deadlocked in the 12th, when the Senators got two men aboard with one out. Earl McNeely hit a grounder to Lindstorm at third, but then lightning struck for the second time. The ball hit another pebble (or was it the same one?) and ricocheted over the hapless Lindstrom's head, delivering Muddy Ruel from second with the winning run.

10.5   D. Roger Peckinpaugh

The AL MVP in 1925, Peckinpaugh was an unlikely candidate for Series goat, but that's precisely what fate had in store for the Senators shortstop. He committed a Series record eight errors, many of them critical ones, as the Pirates rallied from a 3–1 deficit in games to take the Series. Peckinpaugh nearly redeemed himself in game seven, hitting a homer to put the Senators up 7–6 in the eighth, but in the bottom of the inning he bobbled a potential double-play ball, allowing the Pirates to load the bases. The next batter, Kiki Cuyler, then doubled home two runs, as the Bucs went on to win 9–7.

10.6   B. Seventh inning

Once the dominant hurler in the National League, in 1926 Grover Alexander was a nearly deaf, 39-year-old alcoholic who was prone to epileptic seizures. When sober, though, the grizzled Nebraskan could still pitch. "Old Pete" shut out Ruth and the boys at Yankee

Stadium in game two, then beat them again on their home turf in game six, to knot the Series at three games apiece. Thinking his work was done, Alexander went out to celebrate. The deciding game was played the next day in a steady drizzle. Alexander was nursing a hangover in the bullpen when New York, trailing 3-2 in the seventh, loaded the bases with two outs against Redbird starter Jesse Haines. At bat was the dangerous Tony Lazzeri. Sensing impending disaster, manager Rogers Hornsby summoned his old warhorse. Yankee fans fell silent as Alexander ambled in from the bullpen through a gray mist. Hornsby met him on the mound. "Bases filled, eh?" Alexander said casually. "I guess there's nothing to do except give Tony a lot of hell." Hornsby looked in the pitcher's bloodshot eyes and asked him if he was up to the task. "I can try," Alexander responded. The wily veteran fanned Lazzeri on three pitches, then held the Yanks hitless for the last two innings to nail down the win.

10.7   B. Two

The 1927 Yankees possessed an awesome array of bats. After watching Babe Ruth, Lou Gehrig and Bob Meusel launch long bombs into the seats during batting practice before game one, many observers anticipated a massacre. But the Yankee power factory generated only two homers in the Series, both by Ruth. The key to the Yankees' sweep of the Pirates was their pitching. The foursome of Herb Pennock, Waite Hoyt, Wilcy Moore and George Pigras limited the Bucs, who batted a robust .305 as a team during the season, to a paltry .223 average.

10.8   B. Lou Gehrig

Babe Ruth and Lou Gehrig laid waste to the Cardinals pitching staff in 1928, establishing a gaudy array of records for a four-game series. Ruth scored nine times, cracked ten hits, hit three homers (all in one game), batted .625 and amassed 22 total bases. Gehrig scored five runs, hit four homers, had nine RBI, batted .545 and posted an otherworldly slugging average of 1.727. Gehrig's numbers might have been even better if the terrified Cardinal pitchers had not walked him six times, five of them coming in the last two games.

10.9 D. Howard Ehmke

Howard who? That's what many of the Chicago Cubs players were asking when Ehmke was picked by Athletics manager Connie Mack to start the opener of the 1929 Series. The 35-year-old journeyman had appeared in only 11 games in 1929 and had not pitched at all during the last month of the season. But Mack had a hunch that the crafty veteran's off-speed junk might confuse the Cubs' sluggers and had sent Ehmke on the road to scout his opponents during the last few weeks of the season. Mack looked like a genius when Ehmke won 3–1, tossing an eight-hitter and fanning 13 batters to set a Series strikeout record that lasted 24 years. It was Ehmke's last hurrah. He never won another game.

10.10 A. Charlie Root

No one disputes that Babe Ruth came to bat in the fifth inning of the third game of the 1932 Series at Chicago's Wrigley Field and hit a mammoth homer to center field. Likewise, no one disputes that during the at-bat, Ruth responded to a deluge of taunts and curses from the fans and the Cubs' bench with several gestures and remarks of his own. What has never been determined is whether Ruth actually pointed to the spot where the ball landed. Charlie Root, the Cubs pitcher who delivered the fateful pitch, went to his deathbed adamant that Ruth never pointed to the fence. Ruth himself was evasive on the question, saying, "It's in the papers, isn't it?" Most chroniclers agree that Ruth did gesture toward either Root or the Cubs' dugout, but the notion that he was pointing to the bleachers is likely a fabrication of the New York press. None of the reporters at the game initially reported anything unusal about the homer except for his remarkable distance. Still, that does not diminish the feat. As Robert Creamer wrote in his biography *Babe: The Legend Comes to Life*, "He did challenge the Cubs before 50,000 people, did indicate he was going to hit a home run and did hit a home run. What more could you ask?"

10.11 A. Joe Medwick

The St. Louis Cardinals blew open a tight Series with the Detroit Tigers in 1934 by exploding for seven runs in the third inning of the seventh game, en route to an 11–0 whitewash. But what is most memorable about the game is the eruption that occurred in the sixth inning after Joe Medwick hit a triple and slid hard into Tigers third baseman Marv Owen. When Medwick tried to take his position in left field in the bottom of the inning, irate Detroit fans showered him with a barrage of fruit and vegetables. After a 20-minute delay, during which the crowd continued its bombardment, commissioner Kenesaw Mountain Landis ordered Medwick removed from the game to restore order and for his own safety. Recounting the episode years later, Medwick said, "I know why they threw it; what I couldn't figure out is why they brought it to the park in the first place."

10.12 C. 18

When Carl Hubbell, the Giants' ace lefty, tamed the mighty Yankees 6–1 in the opener of the 1936 Series, Giants fans sensed an upset. That illusion was rudely shattered in game two, when the Bronx Bombers savaged five Giants pitchers in an 18–4 massacre. Every player in the Yankees lineup had at least one hit and scored at least one run, as Bill Dickey and Tony Lazzeri paced the onslaught with five RBI each. Eighteen runs remains the most scored in any game in Series history. Although the Giants kept things closer the rest of the way, the Yankees prevailed in six games.

10.13 C. Charlie Keller

The Yankees made it four world titles in a row by sweeping Cincinnati in the 1939 Series. Although the Reds managed to hold the rest of the Yankees in check, they had no answer for rookie right-fielder Keller, who hit a sizzling .438. Called "King Kong" because of his bushy black eyebrows and muscular body, Keller was a one-man wrecking crew. In game one, he tripled and scored the winning run in the ninth. In game two, he scored two of New York's four runs. In game three, he scored three times, hit two homers and had four RBI. In the game four, he hit another homer and scored three runs, the last in spectacular fashion in the tenth inning. Racing all the way home from first on a Joe DiMaggio single and an outfield error, Keller barreled into catcher Ernie Lombardi, jarring the ball loose and knocking the Reds' backstop senseless, enabling DiMaggio to sprint home for the final run in a 7–4 victory. The familiar cry of

"Break up the Yankees" was given a new twist by one Cincinnati fan, who moaned in the aftermath, "Break up the Yankees. Hell, I'll be satisfied if they break up Keller."

10.14 D. He had been the Reds' third-base coach for three years

Under normal circumstances, Jimmie Wilson would never had played in the 1940 Series. Aside from a few nominal appearances, the 39-year-old catcher had retired in 1937 to coach third base for the Reds. However, an ankle injury to first-string catcher Ernie Lombardi and the tragic midseason death of backup Willard Hershberger forced the Reds to reactivate Wilson late in the year. The veteran performed beyond expectations, catching six games, gunning down the only Tiger runner who tried to steal on him, hitting .353 and stealing the only base of the Series, as the Reds took the Tigers in seven games.

10.15 B. Mickey Owen

"The condemned jumped out of the chair and electrocuted the warden," was the way one writer described the Yankees' miraculous comeback in game four of the 1941 Series. The Dodgers were up 4–3 in the top of the ninth, when reliever Hugh Casey fanned Tommy Henrich on a 3–2 pitch for what should have been the game's final out. Unfortunately for the Dodgers, the ball eluded catcher Mickey Owen, allowing Henrich to reach first. Given a reprieve, the Yanks staged a four-run rally to win the game 7–4 and went on to clinch the Series the next day. Ironically, during the season, the sure-handed Owen had set a new NL record for catchers by handling 476 straight chances without an error. But his one crucial miscue in the 1941 Series is all anyone remembers about Mickey Owen today.

Game Answers

Game 1:
What's My Line?
1. Eddie Cicotte
2. Dizzy Dean
3. Casey Stengel
4. Babe Ruth
5. Mel Ott
6. Lou Gehrig
7. John McGraw
8. Satchel Paige
9. Leo Durocher
10. Lefty Gomez
11. Babe Herman
12. Ty Cobb
13. Ted Williams
14. Rabbit Maranville
15. Branch Rickey
16. Rogers Hornsby

Game 2:
Diamond Monikers
1. K
2. H
3. B
4. F
5. A
6. J
7. I
8. G
9. D
10. L
11. C
12. E

Game 3:
Time Travel
1. 1933
2. 1924
3. 1928
4. 1930
5. 1934
6. 1920
7. 1940
8. 1939
9. 1941
10. 1922
11. 1938
12. 1935

Game 4:
The Sultan of Swat
A. 1
B. 1
C. 2
D. 3
E. 12
F. 11
G. 15
H. 123
I. 94
J. 177

Game 5:
Keystone Combos
1. Travis Jackson
2. Tommy Thevenow
3. Mark Koenig
4. Woody English
5. Joe Boley
6. Charlie Gelbert
7. Buddy Myer
8. Billy Rogell
9. Billy Jurges
10. Joe Gordon

Game 6:
Raising the Flag
1. 1927 Yankees
2. 1935 Cubs
3. 1920 Indians
4. 1936 Yankees
5. 1927 Pirates
6. 1930 Cardinals
7. 1931 Athletics
8. 1932 Yankees
9. 1940 Reds

Game 7:
Fabulous Feats
1. George Sisler
2. Jimmie Foxx
3. Tris Speaker
4. Babe Ruth
5. Rogers Hornsby
6. Ted Williams
7. Ty Cobb
8. Lou Gehrig
9. Joe DiMaggio
10. Joe Medwick
11. Hank Greenberg
12. Al Simmons

Game 8:
Great Pretenders
1. Babe Ruth
2. Joe Medwick
3. Mel Ott
4. Al Simmons
5. Rogers Hornsby
6. Carl Hubbell
7. Lefty Grove
8. Earl Averill
9. Joe DiMaggio
10. Babe Herman

ACKNOWLEDGEMENTS

The author gratefully acknowledges the help of photo researchers W.C. Burdick of the National Baseball Hall of Fame, and Jocelyn Clapp of Corbis-Bettmann, editor John Eerkes, designer Peter Cocking, Rob Sanders and Terri Wershler of Greystone Books, Candice Lee, and the many baseball writers whose brilliant prose has helped to illuminate the game.

PHOTO CREDITS

Corbis-Bettmann: pages 58 and 99

National Baseball Hall of Fame Library, Cooperstown, N.Y.: pages 2, 11, 20, 29, 34, 41, 44, 48, 55, 62, 69, 74, 83, 88, 102, 114, 123, and 128.

ABOUT THE AUTHOR

Kerry Banks is an award-winning journalist and sports columnist. He is also the author of *The Glory Years: Old-Time Baseball Trivia,* and the co-author of *Classic Hockey Trivia* and *Ultimate Hockey Trivia.*